S. H. HADLEY'S LATEST PHOTO.

S. H. HADLEY

OF

WATER STREET

A MIRACLE OF GRACE

BY

J. WILBUR CHAPMAN, D.D.

ILLUSTRATED

NEW YORK   CHICAGO   TORONTO

Fleming H. Revell Company

LONDON   AND   EDINBURGH

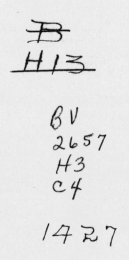

New York :   158 Fifth Avenue
Chicago :   80 Wabash Avenue
Toronto :   25 Richmond St., W.
London :   21 Paternoster Square
Edinburgh :   100 Princes Street

SAMUEL HOPKINS HADLEY, FOR
NINETEEN YEARS AND EIGHT
MONTHS AND TEN DAYS THE
SUPERINTENDENT OF THE OLD
JERRY McAULEY WATER
STREET MISSION, SITUATED AT
316 WATER ST., NEW YORK CITY

NEW YORK CITY, February 26, 1906.
REV. J. WILBUR CHAPMAN, D. D.,
    156 Fifth Avenue, New York City.
    Dear Dr. Chapman—It is the earnest desire of Mrs. S. H. Hadley, and this desire is heartily seconded by the Trustees of Water Street Mission, that you should write the story of the life of our dearly beloved Superintendent and friend, Rev. S. H. Hadley. Will you do this? We feel that of all men you are the one whom our dear friend would have suggested for this work.
    Awaiting your reply, I am,
                    Cordially yours,
                            WALTER M. SMITH.

                    NEW YORK CITY, February 28, 1906.
MR. WALTER M. SMITH, 115 Worth Street, New York City.
    My dear Mr. Smith—I have received your kind letter and beg to say that the request you make of me is indeed a high honour. I accept the work as a great trust. I will do the very best I can and at the earliest possible time I will see that the manuscript is in the publisher's hands, only it is to be understood that I am in no way personally to be profited by the sale of the book, and so far as I am concerned all the profit is to be devoted to Mrs. S. H. Hadley or to the Mission, as the Trustees may direct.
                    Cordially yours,
                            J. WILBUR CHAPMAN.

INTRODUCTION

No man, however gifted, can define the manner in which the Holy Spirit transforms a dying drunkard into a prince among mission workers.

Samuel Hopkins Hadley was so transformed; and, though the process may elude us, the fact is before us. It is before us in this book that tells the story of his life.

Mr. Hadley, when he thought himself to be dying of delirium tremens, was conscious of " a great and mighty presence "; and he never doubted for a single moment that Jesus, the sinner's friend, had come in person to save him. From that hour he was a saved man; and to the day of his death he bore constant and faithful witness to the fact that Jesus, and Jesus only, could save the lost. None that knew him ever questioned his love for the Lord Jesus or the sincerity of his testimony. By that testimony multitudes of Christians were strengthened in faith, and by it multitudes of helpless, dying sinners were led to accept the grace he proclaimed.

Water Street, the scene of his labours, was like a land-locked harbour, into which there was a constant drift of wrecked humanity. Here, night after night, might be witnessed miracles as marvellous as those wrought by the Lord Jesus during His sojourn upon the earth. There is perhaps no place in the world where more soul-thrilling stories of rescue have been told. Christian workers from every part of the globe have been drawn there to hear these marvellous testimonies, to rejoice, to weep, and to go forth with new confidence in the power of God to save.

Chief among these witness-bearers was he of whom these pages treat. I have heard him tell the story of his conversion scores of times. It was always the same, yet always new; always simple, heart-searching and convincing; and always characterised by an intense devotion to his Lord and Saviour.

The sending forth of the life-story of this remarkable man of God will be of untold blessing to believers, and will surely awaken the unconcerned to an apprehension of God's mercy in Christ.

No one better equipped than Dr. Chapman could have been chosen to set forth the great character of which this volume treats. None knew Mr. Hadley more intimately; none loved him more devotedly; none more deeply sympathised with him in his work; none could see more clearly nor estimate more justly the salient features of his life and character.

His book is a great and worthy tribute to one whose devotion to the Lord Jesus Christ gave him a conspicuous place among modern mission workers. It is a witness also to the power of God among men.

No more enduring monument could be erected and in no other way could the influence of a great life be so effectively perpetuated.

In these pages Mr. Hadley still lives and still serves his Redeemer in whose presence he now abides with joy unspeakable and full of glory.

> "God calls our loved ones, but we lose not wholly
> What he has given:
> They live on earth in thought and deed as truly
> As in his heaven."
>
> —Ford C. Ottman.

Stamford, Conn.

PREFACE

To attempt to write the story of the life of S. H. Hadley is an honour and a privilege which anyone might covet. It is impossible for me to have read over the story of his early life, the account of his conversion, and then acquaint myself with the marvellous way in which God used him, without realising that the day of miracles is not passed.

A great Apostle of Unbelief once said, "Show me a miracle which your God has worked and I will believe in Him." If that representative of unbelief were living to-day I should try to tell him the story of the life and work of S. H. Hadley. It is as truly a miracle as the turning of water into wine. He was one of the dearest friends I ever had and one of the noblest souls I ever came in contact with. He was as genuine as the day was long, and when once he gave himself fully to Christ he never swerved an inch from the straight and narrow way. He was the most like Christ of any man I have ever met. His patience with the lost and erring was unexampled, his devotion to his work was an inspiration to all who would make their lives felt for the upbuilding of the cause of Christ. He was truly a great man. Thousands of people rise up to-day to call him blessed. I realise how impossible it is to tell the story of his life on the printed page, and yet I enter upon the task thanking God that I am to be able in some slight way to send his story on for the perusal of those who knew him and loved him, and for the inspiration of those who knew him only slightly and possibly not at all except as a public man, and the beloved Superintendent of the old Water Street Mission.

One of the inspirations of Water Street has always been to me, not simply the fact that it was like a great lighthouse sending its cheering rays out over the troubled sea of life and being used of God to lead many a poor lost drunkard to the harbour of safety, but that it was a work which commended itself to some of New York's most distinguished citizens. Men of large means, men of rare business ability, State officials, distinguished ministers, all counted it a privilege to be numbered among the trustees of the Water Street Mission. When the funeral services at the Mission were concluded, these busy New York men made their way upstairs over the Mission and considered prayerfully the interests of the great work, and then passed the following resolutions:

" The Trustees of the Old McAuley Water Street Mission record the expression of their profound sorrow at the death of the Rev. Samuel Hopkins Hadley, who for nearly twenty years was the beloved and loving Superintendent.

" He served the cause of Christ and helped the wretched, the hopeless and the lost with his whole heart and soul by day and night. He touched the hearts and influenced the lives of all with whom he came in contact, and was ever the welcome guest of rich and poor alike.

" Not one did he ever pass by ' on the other side.' He was a conspicuously successful Rescue Mission

Worker. We, the Trustees of this Mission, bear testimony to his faithful service and esteem it a sacred privilege and honour to have been associated with him."

The above resolutions were adopted by the Board of Trustees at a meeting held on Monday morning, February 12, 1906.

[Signed.]   JOHN S. HUYLER, President,
             R. FULTON CUTTING, Treasurer,
             W. T. WARDWELL,
             W. M. SMITH,
             W. E. LOUGEE,
             M. LINN BRUCE,
             W. S. BOWNE,
             A. N. RYERSON,
             M. HARTLEY DODGE,
             Rev. J. FREDERICK TALCOTT,
             C. F. TIETJEN,
             B. DE F. CURTIS, Secretary.

It is therefore a high honour to write the story of a work, which not only has the seal of God's approval, but the emphatic endorsement of these distinguished men.

                              J. WILBUR CHAPMAN.

Acknowledgment is made to Mr. G. B. T. Davis for the use of the stenographically reported funeral services embodied in chapters sixteen and seventeen.

CONTENTS

LIST OF ILLUSTRATIONS

JAMES C. EDWARDS.

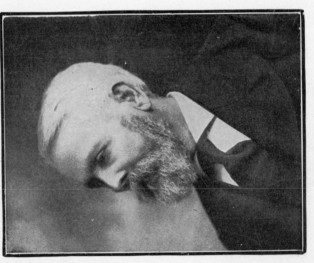

PHILIP McGUIRE.

I

"UNCLE PHIL"

"**W**HO is the aged minister standing at the door?"

I addressed these words one winter evening to S. H. Hadley, the Superintendent of the Water Street Mission at 316 Water street, New York city, as I came up on the platform of the Mission Hall and took my place by his side.

Mr. Hadley was occupying the chair which had been especially dedicated to him for his use and I had the privilege of being seated in an old arm chair which had been occupied so many years by Jerry McAuley, the Founder of the Mission and who was known in his day as the "Apostle to the Outcast."

"Minister?" said Mr. Hadley, rising to his feet and looking about as if he feared that some city pastor or some visiting minister might have entered the Mission unobserved. "I do not see any minister here in the audience." Then I rose and standing beside him said, "I mean the grey-haired, benevolent-looking old man who is just on the right of the door, who is now speaking to the man in rags who has just entered the Mission."

When I said this Mr. Hadley burst into a laugh. "Why, man," said he, "that is not a minister, that's old Phil," and then he said, "We all call him Uncle Phil," and for more than two years afterwards I never knew his name as other than Uncle Phil, but I came to know him later on and to love him devotedly.

I once called him Mr. McGuire and he really seemed offended; at another time I spoke of him as Mr. Philip McGuire and he responded with little enthusiasm; but ever afterwards when I called him "Uncle Phil," his eyes would shine and his face would glow, and whenever I entered the sacred place, Mr. Hadley himself gave me no more affectionate greeting than this wonderful man who had been rescued from so sinful a life and who through all his Christian experience, to strangers, to the outcast, to old men, and to little children, so beautifully exemplified the spirit of the Master who had saved him by His marvellous grace.

Philip McGuire was born in Ireland in 1831. He was brought to New York city while a baby and grew up in the old Fourth Ward. Before he was twelve years of age he had been arrested three times for stealing, and sent as many times to the House of Refuge. Then he ran away from his home and spent the next three years on board a whaling vessel that took him around the globe. He was a born thief, and when he returned from his sailing experience he kept up his life of crime and in all served twenty years in different prisons. He was about as hopeless a case as one could expect to find.

During his second term in Sing Sing he had his place in chapel side by side with Jerry McAuley, the river pirate, who later on started the Mission which has ever since been known as the Jerry McAuley or Water Street Mission. He sat by Jerry McAuley on the day when the latter, after listening to a talk by "Awful" Gardner, declared himself converted and determined to lead a new life ever afterwards. Gardner was a noted character in New York. His name was Orville, but he had always borne the nickname of " Awful," and in the truest sense he lived up to his name. When Jerry McAuley left Sing Sing and McGuire too had been discharged, Jerry brought him down to the Mission. There McGuire tried his best to follow the example set by his former fellow-prisoner, but with small success.

One day when he was in charge of the Mission a stranger entered and placed in his hands a large sum of money, asking that he give it to Jerry when he returned. What was he to do? He was a born thief. This money burned in his hands. He was alone in the Mission. He walked excitedly up and down the room, debating in his mind whether he should steal the money or not, and in the midst of it all Jerry McAuley entered. Phil rushed towards him saying, " Jerry, for God's sake, take this money, for if you don't, I will steal it." McAuley took the money, but McGuire was so shaken by the experience that the next day he stole about twelve dollars from the poor box, which is just on the right of the door as you enter the Mission. Jerry was relentless with a hypocrite, so he sent him back to Sing Sing and for seventeen years afterwards he lived a life of crime.

I can never forget hearing from Mr. Hadley's lips the story of his return to Water Street. He said :

" Old Phil McGuire came into the Water Street Mission one night, so drunk that he could scarcely walk, an old thief sixty-three years of age at that time, who had served over twenty years in different state prisons for burglary. The last thing he did before coming into the Mission was to take off his last shirt in the street and sell it for ten cents, with which he bought two drinks of Fourth Ward whiskey.

"When we invited sinners to come up to our mercy seat he was so drunk the aisle was not wide enough for him to walk in. I helped the old bum down on his knees at our altar service, and also helped him to take his seat, but in that brief time of perhaps five minutes, that mysterious, wonderful being, the Holy Spirit, came into the heart of old Phil McGuire, and from that moment he was another man. He never took a drink, and never wanted a drink till the day of his death."

Shortly after his conversion he gave the following testimony, which was taken down by one who was present:

"Cheer up, boys! Down here we don't think anybody kin git so low that the love of Jesus can't save him. Say, boys, I've got a clean shirt on now, I'm clean shaven, an' what's more, I ain't had a drink fer years an' don't want none. Just the same, it wasn't so long ago I was goin' around like you fellers, drunk on stale beer an' anything else I could git hold of, sleepin' in gutters an' thinkin' nothing could save me. Before that I was even worse. I was a thief, a crook. I did all the things the good Bible says we mustn't do. I done time in Sing Sing an' other places, yet here I am to-night a saved man, hauled right out of a good sight worse fix than any of you boys are in. Did I save myself? Did any drugs save me? No, boys; it was the love of Christ. Nuthin' else can do it. All the making up yer mind ter quit in the world don't help a bit. Yer'll fall again, sure. Take Jesus in and

you're saved. He kin save you, boys, a sight easier
than he saved me, an' he's made a good job of it with
me, too.

" God bless yer, boys, an' God bless Jerry McAuley,
he that started this Mission. They say I'm the only
man alive that was in Sing Sing with Jerry. I met
him there an' we knew each other well. I was a bad
man, but a heap sight worse man was Jerry McAuley.
I didn't take no stock in Jerry's conversion in Sing
Sing, but it was the beginning of his great life for
God.

" Boys, I came out of Sing Sing not long after
Jerry had been pardoned. I was hungry and cold an'
I had the hankerin' for a drink, that they'd tried to
crush out of me in prison. I hadn't a cent, though,
and as I was walking up the Bowery I met Jerry.

" ' What's yer lay, Jerry? ' I asked.

" He laid his hand on my shoulder, looked me in
the eyes, an' said, ' Phil, I ain't on any lay but the
work of Jesus Christ. Come around an' see me, Phil.'

" I went around to see Jerry an' his Mission here,
and he talked to me, fed me, clothed me, and sent me
away thinking. Boys, the change didn't come right
away. It took time for me to see that nothing but the
love of Jesus would save me. I got drunk again and
again after my meeting with Jerry, but every time I
turned up here on Water Street I found Jerry's hand
out to me. Well, boys, the Lord came into me one
night to stay, an' with him coming in every desire for
the old life went out. Oh, boys! if yer could only
know it—know what it means—yer'd grab it so
quick!"

It is the custom in Water Street if one has stood a

year for Christ and been consistent to observe his anniversary. The convert reads the Scripture, offers prayer, and tells of the Saviour's keeping power through the year that is passed.

The following is in substance the testimony of Phil McGuire as he gave it on the night of the fifth anniversary of his conversion, November 23, 1897. Compare these two testimonies and you will see the evidence of his spiritual growth.

After reading the 30th Psalm, he said: "I was always bad. I wouldn't stay home. I would run away. I was a natural thief. Before I was twelve years old I had been arrested three times. Then my father sent me to sea to get rid of me. After that I was worse and worse, arrested many times and while I was serving my second term in Sing Sing State Prison I got acquainted with Jerry McAuley.

"When I left prison I had work for a time, then through drink I lost that and was in hard luck when, one day on Fourth Avenue, I met Jerry and asked him if he could get me a job. He told me to come down to the Mission. I didn't know what a mission was, but I came and heard the man I knew had been a thief tell what Jesus could do and how he had made him honest and sober. That night I went forward for prayers and believe I was saved, but later on I left the mission and after a time went back again. One day I robbed the mission cash-collection box and then Jerry had me sent to prison.

"Seventeen years after I first came here I returned. For days I was trying to 'sober-up' to come here, but I couldn't get sober. The appetite was so strong. So I came in drunk, and staggered to the altar. But I was saved that night and the Lord has kept me ever since. The next day Mr. Hadley gave me twenty-five cents. Twelve cents of this I paid to get my shirt out of pawn and I've never been broke since. I ain't afraid of officers now. When I meet a policeman now he bows to me."

On another occasion Uncle Phil testified: "When I served the devil I was never satisfied. I worked ten years for fifteen dollars a week, and when I was laid off I hadn't money enough to keep me one week. But since I've been serving the Lord I'm always satisfied. Since I began to serve the Lord I was working for 'most three years for five dollars a week and when I got laid off I had money enough to keep me four months and some to spare."

He was perfectly devoted to his Superintendent. One summer when the financial burdens of the Mission were heavier than ever and the demands upon the treasury greater than they had previously been, Mr. Hadley decided to give up his vacation; he determined that he would not even go to Northfield or Winona to attend the Bible Conferences. Uncle Phil found it out; one evening he met him in the Mission and when no one was around he slipped fifty dollars which he had saved, into his hand and said, " Here, take this, go to Winona, don't say anything about it; God bless you," and the old man began to sob. Mr. Hadley came directly to my home and said, " I don't think I was ever more moved in my life than by the devotion of this old man."

In his description of him his Superintendent wrote as follows:

" He was our janitor, lived in our home, ate at our

table, and was loved by us, as a dear member of our own family, faithful as the sun, honest in the least particular as well as the greatest, and I would trust him with uncounted money. Never have I known one penny in the thousands of dollars he handled to go astray."

His death was a remarkable one. Mr. and Mrs. Hadley were away from the Mission one evening, but when the services were all over the Assistant Superintendent bade dear old Phil good-night and went upstairs to retire, leaving him to attend to the wants of the needy ones and close up the place.

Suddenly one of the boys ran hurriedly upstairs and said, " Old Phil is dying." The Superintendent hastened down into the Mission Chapel and found one of the boys holding him on a seat. They prepared to carry him upstairs to his room when he shook his head. Those who stood about him noticed he was restless and with great effort moving his hands, at last they saw that he was trying to get his hands into his vest pockets.

Mr. Hadley had written a book giving an account of his experiences in Water Street. It was entitled, " Down in Water Street," and was sold for one dollar. When strangers visiting the points of interest in New York came to the Mission, the old janitor would frequently sell a copy of this notable book.

His poor fingers were fast stiffening in death, but when those about him realised that he would not be satisfied until he reached his pockets they assisted him. Taking out a dollar bill from one pocket and with almost superhuman effort a like sum of money from another pocket, he stretched forth both his hands and said, "Books," and was gone. The last act of his life was an honest one. He had been saved by the grace of God. The illustration is an inspiration. What God could do for Phil McGuire He can do for lost and wandering men throughout the world.

In writing about his funeral Mr. Hadley said:

"His funeral was a notable event. It occurred on the 18th day of last January. People came for miles to the funeral of the ex-thief Phil McGuire. Reporters from all the great dailies of the city were present. The house was crowded, and I had to close the doors, for more people came than could get in, millionaires and bums, merchants and thieves, beautiful women and harlots. Oh, what a collection you can get into a rescue mission! All came to the funeral of the old ex-thief and drunkard Phil McGuire. Why did all these people come on a cold winter night to such an out-of-the-way place as the Old McAuley Mission?" Because dear old Phil had bound them to him with ties of love that could not be broken.

Before Mr. Hadley went downstairs to attend the funeral service of his old friend he was asked if he did not wish to write something concerning him. He picked up a piece of Water Street stationery and wrote the stanza reproduced on the following page.

If you will multiply many times this story of the genuine conversion of a poor lost man, you will have the life story of S. H. Hadley, the man who during his Christian life possibly led more drunkards to Christ than any other man of his generation. His companions in rescue work certainly agree that of all the rescue mission workers of his day he was easily the greatest, yet he was as humble as a child.

TELEPHONE 4038 JOHN

'Down in Water Street.' A book of thrilling interest of sixteen years' life and work in The Old McAuley Mission. A sequel to the life of Jerry McAuley By S. H. HADLEY, Supt. Address S. H. HADLEY, 316 Water St., New York. Price, One Dollar with 30 illustrations.

New York Jan 18" 1903

Servant of God well done
Thy glorious warfare is past
The battles fought
The victory won
And thou art crowned
at last

— S H Hadley

last tribute to
uncle Phil McGuire

MR. HADLEY'S AUTOGRAPH MEMORANDUM OF STANZA QUOTED BY HIM AT THE FUNERAL OF PHIL McGUIRE.

II

HIS HOME LIFE

THERE are those who have felt that they have known S. H. Hadley at his best when they have seen him in Water Street, leading poor lost drunkards, such as he had been in other days, to Christ. There are others who have thought that he was strongest when he was leading a conference of ministers, for he was bright and witty and always seemed to say the right thing in the right way. There are still others who have suggested that he was at his best when he was met in a social way, but I have no hesitation in saying, that from all I have seen, heard, and read, he really never revealed himself to a better advantage than when he was in his home with his loved ones about him, with a few of his friends of the Mission near him, and best of all, with the very atmosphere of heaven pervading the entire household.

The story of his home life would take us back to the days when he was a boy in the home, where privation and suffering sometimes were necessary, but where love always was supreme. The members of the Hadley household were devoted to each other, and their devotion seemed to grow with the passing years. There came to me recently a letter from his sister, in which she said: " One thing noticed by all who knew him in his childhood days was his tender heart. He could not see anything hurt or witness its suffering without pain. If a fowl was to be prepared for dinner, he could not see it killed. He would run and hide his head in his mother's lap, so that he could not hear the report of the gun. As he grew older and more brave this tenderness never left him. His mother was his idol, and never could he say an unkind word to her. When he was about twenty-five years old he attended a revival meeting at Trimble, Athens County, Ohio. He became very much interested, and with two of his companions confessed Christ and was baptized in the waters of Sunday Creek. He united with the church near my home where the town of Glouster is now situated. He became an active member of the meeting and his presence in prayer and song was a blessing to all. But one day unexpectedly and in an angry moment he swore. Then he thought that all was over and he could be a Christian no longer, so he gave it all up. People wondered what had caused such a sudden change in his life and he himself did not tell it for years. This is one reason I am sure, why he could not give up anyone who ever made a start in the Christian life. He was a darling brother, and the best example of Christ I have ever known."

Not a very great while ago there came into my possession a copy of Lucy Hadley's journal. She was a sister of S. H. Hadley. She was born August 23, 1836, and died November 3, 1879. What she has written has to do with the real home life of S. H. Hadley.

"February 12, 1853.

"My father has lately joined the Presbyterian church, and on the 20th of December, 1852, for the first time in his life erected the family altar in his own house; and commenced asking a blessing at the table. It was a melting time among us that Monday morning. I know I shall never forget it. We sang before prayers this verse:

> " ' Let not despair as fell revenge
> Be to my bosom known
> But give me tears for others woes
> And patience for my own.'

" We sing during family worship every morn and eve, and many sweet sessions have we had together. Mother always prayed with us children every day until father erected the family altar. Oh, I am not half thankful enough for this great blessing."

" February 27, 1853.
" To-day I had the pleasure of seeing my dear brother Henry unite with the Methodist church at Young's Chapel."

" January 1, 1854.
" Last Sabbath was Christmas. We had a very good meeting and I had the pleasure of seeing my youngest brother Hopkins unite with the church at Young's Chapel. May the Lord enable him to be faithful."

" January 16, 1854.
" My longing desire of soul is that my little brothers should become Christians. But the Lord will make them Christians. I feel it; I know it. I feel as sure of it now as if I saw it before my eyes, for the Lord

has promised and *He will* perform. Glory be to God
for this blessed assurance. My soul is full of love."

"February 25, 1854.

"We have just closed a protracted meeting at
Young's Chapel of nearly a week's duration. It has
been a very precious time to many souls. The members have been greatly roused up. There have been
two conversions and five accessions to the church. It
is the first time I ever saw a soul converted in our
meeting house. But I have not yet obtained the longing desire of my heart. I have not yet seen my dear
little brothers converted. Oh, why is it?"

"March 5, 1854.

"I have great reason to serve and love the Lord
for what He has done for me. This morning during
family prayer my dear little brother Hopkins obtained
the witness that he is a Christian. He felt his sins
forgiven, and was enabled to rejoice in the Lord. Oh,
how should my soul swell with gratitude and love to
God, when I see how He is answering my prayers!"

"March 11, 1855.

(When this was written Lucy Hadley was at "Putnam Female Seminary," Zanesville, O., where she
spent about two years, the only schooling she had except the good instruction given her by her brother.)

"Little did I know when I last wrote how soon my
faith would be tried. I received a letter from mother
last week telling me that our entire dwelling and
nearly all it contained, nearly all our provisions, the

barn, and feed for the cattle, had been burned to ashes. Mother is bearing it with true Christian fortitude. Oh, what a blessing to have such a mother! Our friends have been gathering together some clothes to send home. I am going to send all that I can spare of mine."

The one to whom I am indebted for this journal adds this word:

"I remember my mother telling me after this the Hadley family moved into an old log house on the farm. It had been used as a sheep pen for a while. It was fixed up, and when my father saw it a few years later there was the one living room of log downstairs, two unfinished rooms upstairs, a shed kitchen, and a frame room, sometimes used as a parlour, was built on. This was the Hadley home until the parents died and the family scattered—a great change from the pretty country home near Malta."

"June 22, 1856.
"My dear and only sister Hannah was with me at school last winter. With pleasure I watched her improvement, and rejoiced that she was loved by others; for I would rather she would be loved than to be loved myself. Her health was poor so that she could not study very hard, but she improved very much in gentleness, firmness and loveliness of character."

"January, 1856.
"Oh, I have one of the best of mothers and such a

kind good father, too. He is such a good nurse and
was so faithful to me during my sickness. Besides,
I have such a lovely sister and two dear brothers."

"December 20, 1857.

"About six weeks ago my youngest brother Hopkins cut his right knee very badly with an axe. For
about five weeks he has lain in one position without
being able to move but very little; and has suffered
beyond description. I was only with him Thanksgiving Day. He has been dangerously ill some of
the time, but we hope he is better now. We are not
sure that Hopkins is a Christian and our souls have
been burdened with this. Oh, that God would in mercy
hear and answer our prayers. I cannot but believe
He will. I am going home next Thursday and I expect to see my dear and only sister Hannah married
before I return. I am to be her bridesmaid."

When Uncle Hopkins cut his knee a company of
young people were on their way to the wedding of
Amanda Fowler and Joel Allen (still living in Glouster, O., old and broken).

Other young people, not invited, for fun put
branches of trees across the road to hinder the wedding party. Uncle Hopkins, still quite young, had
no girl with him, so he had to lift the branches out of
the way. They came to one big log which he could
not lift, and in trying to chop it away, the axe slipped
and his knee was cut, even the bone itself being cut.
It was sewed up by the country physician, and he was
allowed to hobble around on it for a day or so, then
when the stitches pulled out, and it was greatly in-
flamed, the doctor ordered him to bed. Toward the

last they called Dr. Hufford, whom he had faith in and wanted. He was a wicked man and grandparents did not want him on that account, but a well-read physician. He lay with his knee bent so it could never be straightened.

"May 27, 1860.

"From my earliest religious life, I have felt this deep love for ministers and missionaries, and oh, the yearning of my soul is to spend my whole life in the cause of the Lord."

After a summer's vacation at home she writes:

"It was so hard for me to leave the dear ones at home. I know I am missed now more than I ever was. Brother Henry and I became more truly acquainted with each other, and we had each other's confidence more fully than ever before. He misses me so much, and mother, dear mother, misses me more than all the rest. She leaned her head on my breast and wept like a child when we parted. I felt as though I could never leave her; but go, I must, and with a great effort I tore myself away from those dear ones. Oh, they all miss me. Father, oh, he seemed to love me more this time than he ever had, and he was always *such a kind father*. And Hopkins was the same dear brother."

"August 23, 1862.

"My brother Henry felt it his duty to go (to war), and he is now in Circleville. The house seemed so lonesome, just as though there had been a funeral in it."

"February 1, 1863.

"I have been appointed superintendent of the Sabbath school here (Young's Chapel). I feel the responsibility to be great, but God gives me strength to bear the burden. Oh, that Hopkins were a better boy. He is the greatest sorrow I have. Lord, save him."

"Feby. 19, 1863.

"On the 17th of February Brother Henry came home from the army. He was the most pitiable looking object I ever saw, reduced by disease to a mere skeleton, with an abscess on his right ankle, not able to walk one step, with scarce strength enough to keep life in his body."

(Henry's father helped to nurse him, but he took sick with a severe attack of lung fever, from which he died March 9, 1863, a little over six months after the death of his wife. Harry and Hopkins were both sick; but Hopkins was able to stand with his sisters beside his bed when he died. William Hadley and Jane Riddell Hadley are buried in Young's Chapel graveyard. Neither of the boys, Henry or Hopkins, could ever go to the cemetery after their father's funeral. Hopkins was very sick the night after the funeral and for several weeks with typhoid lung fever.) "We feared for his life; but God spared him to us."

When S. H. Hadley went to live with his brother, the Colonel, although he was by no means the master of himself as regards his appetite for strong drink, yet he was the same loving and lovable brother. I am told they had a common purse in the family—

that whichever brother was at home felt himself, so long as he had a penny, under obligation to pay the bills of the other. Mrs. Colonel Hadley, in writing to me since his death, said: "He was the dearest brother that ever lived, always thoughtful of us, always bright and cheery; even in the dark days of his awful sin he could not but be loving and kind to us. When he was converted, he just as naturally turned to the home of his brother, as the needle turns to the pole star. It was from his brother's window that he looked forth the first day of his Christian life when he said: 'The birds seem to sing differently, the foliage is different, the street cars seem to me like chariots, and men and women as they pass along the streets seem to have their voices keyed to sweet music.'"

He has ever counted it a pleasure and a privilege to turn away from his busy New York life and go back again to his old Ohio home, where he might have fellowship with his sisters. As a rule, for the past ten years, he has gone each summer from my own home to Ohio, and when the day of his departure for his visit with his sisters would come, he would be as eager as a child to see them. But S. H. Hadley was really at his best in his own home, so dear to him, in rooms over the old Mission at 316 Water Street. He had tried living elsewhere, and with his great ancestry back of him, and enjoying beautiful things as he did, it would have been perfectly natural for him to have delighted in a home in a different part of the city, but the experiment was never a success, and he turned back again to the old Mission. He used to say to his friends: " I wish you would come and see me in my home—it's perfectly beautiful "—and it was. The carpets were not so fine, the pictures, to one who did not know their history, were exceedingly common, the furnishings plain in the extreme, but as you mounted the stairs to his room, every step seemed to bring you nearer heaven, and as you entered the living-room it seemed always as if you were stepping into the presence of God, while to go into his little workroom, or "office," as he called it, was to those who knew him and loved him like entering into the sacred precincts of the Holy of Holies. S. H. Hadley was a man of God, he walked and talked with God, and no one ever came into touch with his great life who did not come away with a benediction. His home was as free as the air to all his friends. "There is always a place for you at my table," he would say, "and if you will let me know when you are coming, I will put your name in the pot, but whether you send me word or not, just come, and you will make me very happy." His clever and devoted wife presided over his table like a queen. It would have been perfectly natural for her to have felt many times that in giving up her noble husband to a work which was so full of trial at times and in constant association with those who had come to the end of all their resources, she was making more of a sacrifice than the world had a right to expect of her, but she did not complain. Many a poor lost man found his way to Christ under her guidance and many a convert of the Water Street Mission declares that it was Mrs. Hadley's gentle words of counsel that turned his thoughts back again to his mother and was the means of his conversion.

This chapter would not be complete without a mes-

MRS. S. H. HADLEY.

sage from Mrs. Hadley herself. At my earnest solici-
tation she has written as follows:

" In the twenty-four years of my husband's conversion I have had some experiences myself. I was
in Washington at the time of his conversion. Had
gone to Baltimore for the wedding of a favourite niece
of mine. And from there to Washington to see my
precious mother, then over eighty years old.

" Well, one morning, I think it was Monday, I received a letter telling me the joyful news that he had
found the Saviour. I was stopping with a very dear
friend at the time. I went into the parlour and closed
the door and read my letter. I was surprised, I
walked the floor, I shouted, I cried, I prayed, I
laughed, and dear Aunt Lue came down and said,
' What is the matter with my girlie.' I exclaimed,
' Oh, Aunt Lue, Mr. Hadley says he is converted, do
you believe it?' She had her arms around me and
we looked each other in the eyes. She said, ' He says
so, does he not, Mittie?' I said, ' Yes.' ' Well, so do
I,' she said. I loved her before, but I think I loved
her ten times as much afterwards. *True friend.* Well,
I do not think there was ever a man watched so closely
as he was. He made a good confession from the
start.

" I found after my return to New York in going to
the Mission every night, I became deeply interested
in the work. It was an entirely new thing to me.
Though I had been a Christian for years, we knew
nothing at all about Mission work as it was done in a
Rescue Mission, where all sorts, all classes, and all
conditions came in. It was a revelation to me, and
then Jerry was a revelation. I can see him before my

mind's eye at this time raising his hand and saying,
' Who will come to Christ to-night? ' Well, my husband was not a lazy Christian, but a working one.
How I praise God for that; he always had a burden
for souls. How well I remember when we went to
housekeeping in three rooms, he would bring poor
fellows to our humble home and take out his last
shirt, socks, and collar and tie, and dress the man up
and take him to the Home in Eighty-sixth Street for
intemperate men and I would gather up the debris on
a shovel and throw it into the fire. How many times
I have done that I could not tell; it seemed to me he
was all the time investing in shirts, collars, and ties,
but it was all right; and then his first lodging house.
We had four rooms there, and we wanted a room
for the Lord. We had one good chamber and I gave
it up for anyone he would bring in with delirium tremens. I put my bed in my sitting-room and we would
have our meals there and entertain all our, or his, company there. We had a very humble home, but a very
happy home, because God was there and Love was
there. I could not tell how many cases he nursed
through the dreadful sickness, but some were nursed
through three times, and then, when they were well,
he would bring them in to my table, that would be the
only time I would see them. The door had been taken
off and it had been boarded up, so there came a time
when I thought I might have the room. Well, I asked
the Lord about it; told him if there were not any more
cases in so many weeks I would take it as an answer
to prayer I was to have the room. I told Mr. Hadley
some day he would come home and find the door open;
so the time passed and no one came, and one day I

opened the door, and we had the room papered and
painted and moved our bed into the room. My husband told me if I would live there until the lease ex-
pired he would furnish me a flat uptown, so before
it did he sold the place out, and we went uptown to live
in Seventy-sixth Street. We had a very comfortable
home and from there, after we had been there three
months, we had a call to Water Street Mission. He
came home one day about noon and said, ' Lizzie,
what do you think about going down to Water
Street?' I said, ' What, to the service to-night?' He
said, " No, I have a call to go to Water Street, to take
charge. What do you think about it?' I thought
over it a while and said, ' Dear, if you have a call to
Water Street, it will be the call of your life.' My
Bible was lying on the table by me, and I said, ' Let
us see what the Word says.' I opened it to the 58th
Chapter of Isaiah, and my eyes rested on the seventh
verse. ' Is it not to deal thy bread to the hungry, and
that thou bring the poor that are cast out to thy house?
When thou seest the naked that thou cover him; and
that thou hide not thyself from thy own flesh?' I
said, ' Dear, there is thy commission.' Then we got
down on our knees and told the Lord about it, and said,
' If we were to go, all right; and if not it was all right
also.' So on the last Sabbath in May, 1886, we went
and he held his first service and James Edwards came
forward. He was a terrible looking object, but Mrs.
Stephen Merritt knelt on one side of him, and I on the
other. We put in his mouth the prayer, ' Lord, be
merciful to me a sinner, for Jesus' sake. Amen.' He
prayed that prayer and has been a sober man ever
since. Twenty years of soul-saving agony for souls,

what an experience, and what a work! all classes, all conditions, have knelt at those benches, and what trophies for the Master! how many have gone home to be forever with the Lord; some have failed—we all come short sometimes—for after we have *done all,* we still are unprofitable servants. For twenty years we gave our lives, our time, ourselves, our all for souls; sometimes, I thought someone else ought to take a turn at it, but I was asked if I thought the Lord had sent us there. I said, ' Yes, I am sure He did.' ' Well, do you think He is sending you away? Pray over it.' And I was sure He was not, only the flesh was getting weary, and I would take up my staff and go forward and press into the thickest of the fight until my health broke down. But I never lost my interest in *my boys, dear fellows.* I never see a poor lost drunkard but my heart goes out to God in prayer for him. There are some cases I would like to tell about, some of the boys that worked for Mr. Hadley in his house at 206 Bowery. It was, he said, one of the worst houses when he bought it, a terrible place, so much so that he bought himself a revolver, there were such desperate men. So there came a time when he said to me, ' Lizzie, I do not think I am a very good Christian.' ' Why not?' said I. ' Well, here I am a Christian and am carrying a revolver. What is my religion worth?' He laid it down on the table and said, ' I will never carry one again.' ' Well,' I said, ' the Lord is mighty to deliver you '—and he gave it up instantly.

" ' Does it pay?' I think so, for after twenty years' work, broken down in health, lame, and growing old, I can say it pays, and if I had my life to go over again I would try to do better work. I could not give any more for I gave my all. My precious husband, all health, strength, everything. Sometimes I would be asked how I could bear the sacrifice, but I tell you truly, I never thought I had made any. I was simply doing what I could in His name, after calling me. I know it was not of our seeking, for until my husband was converted I did not know what a mission was, and to us it was simply marvellous how we were led. Truly, in paths we knew not of and in ways that were marvellous, so I praise the name of the Lord forever and forever.

"I never thought my precious husband would be taken, and I left, but it is another of the ways we know not of, and I just want to say from my inmost soul, 'not my will, but Thine be done, O Lord.'"

There was a fitting climax to his home life. When they carried his precious body from the undertaker's rooms that he might lie in state in his living-room above the Mission, those who knew him most intimately came to look upon him and bathe his upturned face with their tears and appreciation. On Sunday evening, as his loved ones were keeping watch over the sacred remains, there came a stranger up the stairs, a man who had known better days. Under the instruction of S. H. Hadley, at another time, he had caught a glimpse of the Saviour, but the tide of an awful temptation swept him from his feet, and he drifted out into the darkness of despair. But when he heard that S. H. Hadley was dead, he was sobered, and he came to the Mission and asked permission to go up and look upon his precious face. Staggering into the room because of his weakness and his grief, he threw himself upon the coffin and sobbed out: " S.

H. Hadley, when he was living, gave me a vision of Jesus, and now that he is dead, I want to see Him once more."

To me his life was one magnificent picture. There were dark clouds in it, but these clouds only served to make the brighter that part of his life that was so filled with Jesus. I have no hesitation at all in saying what I many times in this book repeat—that I consider him in any walk of his life the most Christlike man I have ever known.

III

TWO BROTHERS

IT would be impossible to write the story of the life of Samuel Hopkins Hadley and not take into account the almost equally interesting story of his beloved brother, Colonel H. H. Hadley, who, in his day, was one of the most remarkable rescue mission workers in the world, for many years supported by the St. Bartholomew Church, New York City, and the superintendent of the St. Bartholomew Mission, the organizer of the Church Army in America, and one who has the distinction of having founded more Rescue Missions than any other man in the world. These two brothers were passionately devoted to each other, and their life-story is so intertwined that the history of either would be incomplete without reference to the other.

William Hadley and his bride began their wedded life at Malta, Morgan County, Ohio, four miles above McConnellsville. There, 'mid their struggles to secure a living from Mr. Hadley's salt wells and the river-bottom farm, six children were born. Number five was a long, gaunt, bony, yellow-skinned, black-haired, dark-eyed boy. When he was three days old, his father, happening to come into the room, found the mother crying as if her poor heart would break.

" Mother, what is the trouble? "

" Oh, he's so homely! " she sobbed.

"Homely? Mercy, no! Why, he'll be a president some day;" and the father named him Henry Harrison Hadley.

When number six was born, the mother named him after her own dear brother, Samuel Hopkins, who was one of the early graduates of Yale College.

The sixth child born to Mr. and Mrs. William Hadley is the subject of this sketch and beyond all question one of the most remarkable men of his generation.

The early home of the Hadleys was a home of privation. These refined, educated New England people endured hardships indeed in the training of their children. There was not a cabin in sight of their home, nor a public road within sixteen miles. They lived in a great four-roomed house which was the pride of the township. A patch of ground was cleared about the house; all of the Hadley children helped to pick the brush and clear the land. Gradually the country was settled, log schoolhouses were built, and the educational work of the State was started. While the children of the average frontiersman could scarcely be spared from the farm, Harry and Hopp (as S. H. Hadley was called in his boyhood days) were sent four months in each year to the log schoolhouse. These boys never knew what it was to have a holiday. When they were not busy they were taught by their mother, whose constant fear seemed to be that her boys would grow up in ignorance or adopt the ways of the rough people around them with whom they were compelled to mingle. Their boyhood days were spent in the purest home imaginable.

Not a day was their education neglected by their parents. At night they would lie on the rough puncheon floor, in front of a great wood-stove and study their lessons. The Hadleys were too poor to burn candles unless absolutely necessary. The boys would tear off hickory splinters from the wood that lay near the stove, and running them under the stove-door, would light them and use them as a sort of torch by the glimmer of which they would catch a sentence from their books, then memorise it in the dark. By the light of another splinter they would read a new sentence or review the old one.

The two brothers were never separated; they worked, planned, studied, and slept together. They grew to be young giants, and woe betide the crowd that would pick a fuss with one of the Hadley boys! Harry once had a fight at recess at school with Sam Hook, over Vine Hazleton. Both boys were about fifteen and both sought the smiles of sweet Levina. They fought it out in a "ring" composed of all the scholars. They were parted finally, but Sam had a badly bitten finger, and Harry religiously bit a red onion every morning before breakfast, all unbeknown to his mother, so that Sam's finger would not heal— and it didn't until Harry quit biting the onion.

When Lincoln was elected President and Fort Sumter had been fired upon, the President of the United States called for 75,000 volunteers. When the second call was made for men to serve for three years, or during the war, Harry Harrison Hadley was one of the first to enlist. On the morning of the awful day that Harry was to leave home for the first time, he and his brother, chum and playmate, went alone into the "spare room." They both broke down and lay upon the floor, clasped in each other's arms. They were strong young men, but they sobbed bitterly. This was the first parting between Henry and Hopkins. Oh, such a parting! Of course Hopp would have gone along but for his lame, stiff knee. Otherwise he was a Hercules in strength, and though shorter than his brother, his arms were an inch longer, and his sledge-like fists had often split an inch poplar board.

So devoted were these brothers that S. H. Hadley never could stay away from the young soldier. Several times he visited him during the service. Once at Paducah, Kentucky. Here he contracted smallpox, and Henry, knowing if it were discovered, his brother would be sent to the pesthouse, which meant almost sure death, kept him in his room, nursing him and sleeping with him every night; but he was discovered after all and sent to the pesthouse. There his brother, now a professional scout, and having the rank of captain, armed to the teeth, visited him in the night, at the risk of his life, furnished him money and delicacies. All through the war their affection seemed to grow until there really seemed to be no bounds to it.

It was my privilege one summer to invite them both to the Winona Bible Conference. They occupied the same room together in the hotel, and when the Conference was over S. H. Hadley said to me, " This has been one of the greatest experiences of my life. My brother and I have scarcely slept half the nights. We have talked over the old incidents of our early life and lived our experiences over until we have almost imagined that we were boys again back in Perry County, free as birds and happy as boys could be with such devoted parents as God has given to us."

Colonel H. H. Hadley, after various business experiences in the Middle West, came to New York in 1868. From the first day he talked of his brother Hopp, and wished that all his friends might have the privilege of meeting him.

In March, 1870, Colonel Hadley became engaged to the young lady whom he afterwards married. His boarding house was not far from the home of his intended wife. He sent to Zanesville, Ohio, for his brother to come on after he had succeeded in getting him a good position in an insurance company. He came to Brooklyn, boarded with the Colonel, and the three, Colonel Hadley, the young lady to whom he was engaged, and S. H. Hadley, from that time were inseparable. Many evenings were spent together in singing the old hymns of the Church. The boys both loved music and could sing sweetly. The Colonel and his intended wife became Episcopalians, but S. H. Hadley did not care for the form and generally went to hear Dr. T. DeWitt Talmage preach. He and the Colonel both drank, but up to that time were rarely seen intoxicated.

H. H. Hadley was married July 13, 1870. They wanted Hopkins to be the best man, but always sensitive about his lameness, he refused; however, he was there and helped to make the evening very happy. He was handsome, bright, witty, and musical, popular with young and old of both sexes.

The first home of the newly married couple was in Newark, New Jersey. To this home Hopp had a night key and the three who were so devoted to each other had a happy time together, only the brothers drank too much and their friends, especially their sisters, Lucy McCann and Hannah Allen, wrote to

them every week in which they had much to say about
their dear brothers' habits.

In 1872 S. H. Hadley met the young lady to whom
he was afterwards married, Miss Sarah Hulse by name.
At the time of their meeting she was about sixteen
years of age. His friends were glad to hear of his
engagement. They especially said that the responsibility of a wife would make him careful. After a while
he became so reckless and was drinking to such excess
that the Colonel advised his returning to Zanesville
to his sister and her husband, both of whom had always
been devoted to the Hadley brothers. He returned to
Ohio. When his brother secured him another position
in New York he came back, and on July 23,
1874, he was married to his first wife. She was not
quite eighteen years of age. They were a handsome
young couple and seemed devoted to each other. The
first Mrs. S. H. Hadley joined Dr. DeWitt Talmage's
church in Brooklyn, and he went with her but still
continued drinking and worked at his business with
difficulty. The 18th of May, 1875, a delicate little son
came to them. The mother was very seriously ill. The
boy was named for his brother, Henry Harrison Hadley.[1] The serious illness of the young mother continued; there had to be nurses, doctors, consultations,
and days of great anxiety. Hopp finally gave up his
business. He was broken-hearted. In the month of

---

[1] This son survives his father. His devotion to his father
was wonderful and his sorrow at his great loss is pathetic.
He has entered into active Christian work since his sorrow
and there are those who are praying that God may raise him
up to do a work similar to that to which S. H. Hadley gave
his life.

MR. HADLEY'S SON, H. H. HADLEY.

S. H. HADLEY AT NINETEEN.

July the end came and the young mother passed away.
The little home was sold out at auction and the young
wife of nineteen was buried. The little son was taken
to the home of his maternal grandparents in the State
of New Jersey. The brothers at this time removed
to Washington, the Colonel opened a law office and
Hopkins went into the insurance business with a desk
in his brother's office. From this time on his moral
descent was rapid. He neglected business, played
cards a great deal, and became generally a fast man of
the world. In 1876 S. H. Hadley became acquainted
with his present wife in the city of Washington. In
1879 they were married. The Colonel, in the mean-
time, had returned to New York City, and in 1880 Mr.
and Mrs. Hadley came on to New York to spend the
summer with the Colonel and his family in their summer cottage. The Colonel was in politics and Hopp
had a position that he got for him, but which he had
great difficulty in keeping. Following this a position
was found for him in which he was supposed to secure
subscriptions to a certain book. It was at this time
that he forged the names that he has so frequently
spoken about. He wrote them in his order book to
keep his position and get his salary. From this point
his descent was more than rapid. It was impossible
for him to hold a position. He was a confirmed drunkard. Through all these years of his dissapation his
devoted wife, the present Mrs. S. H. Hadley, who is
still living and maintaining her interest in the Water
Street Mission, never for a moment deserted him.
She has from the first day of their marriage until this
present moment been his staunch helper and supporter.
It means much to so refined a nature to give up all

that would be pleasing to her in the way of surroundings and devote all her time and energy to the reclaiming of poor lost men and women, but this this noble woman has ever been willing to do. She has lived in the midst of her husband's work. Whenever he came across a fallen girl who needed a friend, he knew that she could find a friend in his wife. While he was away on his mission work, which sometimes kept him into the small hours of the night, she would wait his coming, greet him with a word of cheer, and when the day of awards shall come, and S. H. Hadley receives his crown, there will also be a reward of inestimable value for the noble woman who loved him when there was nothing in him that was lovely, and who never lost step as she marched by his side from the direst of distress to the great position of honour and influence which in his latter days he was able to reach.

The climax of the devotion of these two brothers was the conversion of the Colonel, which is best told in his own language.

"On July 26, 1886, at midnight, I entered a saloon at the corner of Third Avenue and One Hundred and Seventieth Street, and with a lawyer, who was also a heavy drinker, had six brandy cocktails. I had been drinking terribly all day, but it seemed as if every drink made me strangely sober. I had fifty-three drinks that day and night. I feared I would drop dead.

"The lawyer and I grasped hands and took a solemn oath that we would never touch another drop. I meant it, but had often meant it before. I walked home and sent for a physician.

" The lawyer drank again within a week, and was buried within a year.

" On the 28th I again went out to try the hopeless and oft-repeated task of living without strong drink. My business took me down town, and on my way back in the evening, trembling in every nerve, with a thirst no man can describe, I concluded to call at the McAuley Mission and see my brother, who was then superintendent, himself a saved drunkard. I never failed at such times to get sympathy from him and also from my wife. Strange as it may seem, neither of them ever scolded or complained, and though almost discouraged, they prayed and waited. Oh, was faith ever so tried?

" My brother was delighted to see me and persuaded me to remain for the meeting. As I sat there listening to the testimonies, I thought of how true he had been for more than three years, and what a hopeless drunkard he used to be. Then a Scotch printer arose and told how he had been saved from the very gutter, and pointing to his well-dressed, happy wife and little girl, said that they had been compelled to leave him, but now were restored, all because he had accepted Christ as his Saviour.

" All at once it occurred to me that possibly I might be saved, too, if I were to stop trying to do it all myself, follow Jesus and trust Him, and I determined right then to test His power and love.

" I stood up and told the condition I was in, and then coming forward with all my sin, I fell down on my knees at the bench in front and cried to God with all my heart for mercy and forgiveness. I determined then that I would live a Christian life the remainder of my days, whether I felt forgiven or not. I remembered then that mother once told me that if a person dies while earnestly praying to God they would not be lost. Here seemed to me at last a chance for heaven. I would pray till I died, and then surely I would be saved. As I asked God to forgive me for the sake of His dear Son, I felt that Jesus died for me alone. How real it seemed! I could almost hear them driving the great spike nails into the rough cross through his hands. I confess that as I entreated God to take away the terrible appetite for drink, I had not much faith. It had been fed and growing for twenty-four years; had controlled me asleep and awake. So my faith was weak then, if I had any at all.

"Then I thought, 'Well, He bore all that agony for me on the awful cross, and I'll bear this thirst as long as I live.' Soon as that thought entered my mind, it was precious, and I felt a bond of sympathy between the Saviour and me, even me, and said, 'Oh, yes, Lord Jesus, I will gladly bear it all for Thee.' I did not pray any more to have it removed, but that He would comfort me for bearing it with His strength.

"As Brother Smith, the Assistant Superintendent, prayed, I felt resigned, and with a fixed purpose to see the end of a Christian life, took my seat. Somehow I had lost my load; I could feel sad no longer, and from that moment to this I have had no desire, longing, or thirst for alcoholic beverages.

> "'Free! free! the joyous light of heaven
> Comes with full and fair release,
> O God! what light! all sin forgiven,
> Jesus, mercy, love and peace.'

COL. H. H. HADLEY.

"Surely I was turned into another man. I was controlled by the habit of profanity until then, but since have not thought an oath.

"That must have been a happy night for my dear brother. He accompanied me far on my way home and seemed loath to leave me. When I reached home and told my wife, who was anxiously watching, as she had so often done before, she said:

"'You need not have told me, darling boy. I knew it when you came in; now, I shall call you good Henry.'

"Oh, the tears of joy that night! When at last I slept, I dreamed I was in the Mission singing the hymn they sang that night:

> "'I have found repose for my weary soul,
>   Trusting in the promise of the Saviour.
> A harbor safe when the billows roll,
>   Trusting in the promise of the Saviour.'

"The next morning I awoke singing. I felt that I was free. The birds never sang so sweetly as then, and the very rocks seemed to wear smiling faces for me, poor, wicked, sinful me, the chief of sinners, but saved, forgiven, redeemed, converted sure enough this time.

"It was no trouble to keep out of saloons then, nor has it ever been since. I know God can keep me in a saloon, but He does better, He keeps me out of one. No man who loves God likes to go into a saloon!

"My first testimony was given next morning to a brewer, who insisted on my taking a drink.

"'No, I was converted last night,' said I.

"'What's that?' said he. And then I told him all

about it, and that I would never enter a saloon again or touch a drop of strong drink.

"'Well,' said he, shaking my hand, 'I'm glad for the sake of your boys, but just come in and have a sodawater or a cigar.'

"'No,' said I, and from that day to this I've kept off temptation ground, and soon after stopped the use of tobacco.

"I immediately committed myself in all possible ways. Through the columns of my paper, which had been largely devoted to beer and liquor interests, I informed its readers that the editor was converted, and would no longer receive advertisements of saloons and brewers; thus throwing away many hundred dollars yearly which came from that source. It was a severe struggle, but I had decided that Christ and I would live this life together, cost what it would. Oh, how tenderly and beautifully He has redeemed every promise! I was determined to trust Him absolutely, and am very glad that I did, for it has proved His promises and given me wonderful faith."

IV

HIS LIFE STORY

IT is impossible for one to give a more accurate description of the life story of Mr. Hadley than that written by himself in his book, "Down in Water Street."

"I was born in Malta Township, Morgan County, on the banks of the Muskingum River, August 27, 1842, the youngest of six children. My father was a New Hampshire man, who went West when young to seek his fortune. My mother was the daughter of a Congregational clergyman in Massachusetts. Her only brother, Samuel Hopkins Riddell, after whom I am named, was also a clergyman. My grandmother on my mother's side was a Hopkins.

" Her father founded the Hopkins Academy in Old Hadley, Mass. On my mother's side I am a direct descendant of the famous divine, Jonathan Edwards.

" After my mother's education was finished she, too, went to Ohio to teach. My father was a partner of the Buckinghams, of Zanesville and Putnam, Ohio. He afterwards moved to Malta, and bored two salt wells there. He failed in the great crisis of 1837, but had invested for my mother and bought a section of land from the Government in Perry County adjoining.

" There father moved with his family in the dead of winter, in 1845. We moved into a log house in the ' forest primeval ' that surrounded us. This section

of land lay on the dividing ridges of Sunday Creek
and Monday Creek, in Salt Lick Township, Perry
County, Ohio.

" In our log-cabin home I could lie on my bed and
see the stars through the cracks of the roof, and feel
the snow sifting down upon my face in the winter
time. We were lulled to sleep by the barking of foxes
and the hooting of owls in the woods around us, and
were awakened in the morning by the chattering of the
grey squirrels near our windows. From my earliest
recollection I was raised to clearing land; helping to
get our large farm under cultivation. The heft of
the work devolved upon my elder brother, Henry H.,
and myself. My oldest brother, William, died in the
university at Delaware, Ohio, as he was about to finish
his education.

" I had two sisters living, older than myself, Lucy
Hopkins and Hannah Eastman. The eldest child, a
girl, died in infancy. My sisters were converted in
the old log meeting-house which my beloved father
built and gave to the Methodist Episcopal Church,
which was dedicated as ' Young's Chapel,' after the
celebrated Methodist preacher, the Rev. Jacob Young,
D. D. They were about twelve years old when they
were marvellously saved at the ' mourners' bench,'
and received a definite baptism of the Holy Spirit.
The eldest, Lucy, died in 1879. She prayed for me
until the last. Shortly before her death she said to
her husband:

" ' Robert, Hopp will be saved.'

" ' How do you know?' said he, who was at that
time an unbeliever.

" ' Because Jesus told me so,' she said.

" My younger sister, Mrs. Hannah E. Allen, is living to-day, surrounded by her children and grandchildren.

" The neighbourhood in which we lived was very primitive; entirely a farming section. Most of the people lived in log cabins, and opportunities for education were very meagre. I attended school altogether about four months, in the old log schoolhouse with puncheon floors, one whole side of the house being used as a fireplace.

" In this log-cabin home we were brought up to fear God. Family worship was strictly observed morning and evening. I shall never forget the influence of that home; that sweet Christian mother, precious, gentle, and tender. Brought up amid refinement, unused to hard work, out there in our frontier home she did all the work with the aid of us children.

" No whiskey or tobacco ever invaded the sacred precincts of our log-cabin home. I promised my mother as early as I can remember, when being taught my first prayers at her blessed knees, that I never would drink. Indeed, I promised her that before I ever knew what the evils of liquor were. Often in her busy cares, as she would pass by me, she would stop and hug me to her bosom, and say:

" ' My darling boy, you never will drink, will you?' As I would look into her lovely face, I would say:

" ' No, mother, I will never drink.'

" This promise I kept until my eighteenth year, when I was induced to take my first drink. A friend of ours, a man some years older than myself, a prominent business man, had been to town. He got quite drunk, and had a bottle of whiskey with him. I met him on the big road. It was a beautiful moonlight evening, and he stood there perhaps half an hour coaxing me to take a drink, the bottle in one hand and a corn-cob stopper in the other.

"'Come, come, Hopp,' he said, 'do take a drink; now be sociable.'

"'No,' I said, 'I can't drink with you.' I didn't say, as I should have done, that I had promised my mother I never would drink.

"'Come,' said he, 'if you don't drink with me, I will think that you feel yourself above me.' I felt stung at this, and took the bottle from his hands and turned it up, and with my eyes on the moon, which was looking so kindly down on me, I took my first drink.

"Dear reader, I have been careful in making this statement complete, as this was the most critical act of my life up to that time. That first drink changed my whole life. Within ten minutes it seemed to me that I was taken possession of by demons. Thoughts came crowding into my mind to which I had been an entire stranger. Oh, the sorrow and shame and crime and suffering that were entailed as direct results of that first drink!

"It isn't the last drink that hurts a man, or the fourth, or fifth, but the first drink—that is what ruins a man. If these pages are read by one who has not taken his first drink, take counsel by one who has suffered so much, and die before you take it. Let the saloon door be the dead-line to you.

"Within a week from that first drink I could drink half a pint of whiskey right down. My precious mother died shortly after this without having known that I had broken my promise. She was sitting in her chair when the angels came for her, and she said to my sisters, who were standing by: 'Tell Hopkins to meet me in heaven.'

"Yes, dear mother, by the grace of God I will meet you there.

"Six months afterwards my father died, and our home was broken up. I went to study medicine in a village near by, with one of the most prominent physicians in our county. He was a brilliant man, but a drunkard, and what I didn't know before, he taught me. Before my course was finished, I got into trouble through drink, and had to clear out as fast as my horse could go: and, in fact, I kept clearing out for some years afterwards in pretty much the same way from every place that I settled.

"I gave up my studies and became a professional gambler. For fifteen years I rarely went to bed sober. For many years I did not see my danger, or was too much under the influence of liquor to think seriously on the subject. Occasionally, however, ominous forebodings would arise in my heart and I wondered what the end would be.

"In 1870 it grew entirely too hot for me out West, and I came to New York. Through the influence of my brother, Colonel H. H. Hadley, who was here and who stood high in life insurance circles, I obtained a position with a salary of $300 per month and a liberal allowance for expenses. The failure of the company I was with threw me out of a position, and I never was able to command as good a salary afterward.

"I wish I could describe the remorse and heartaches of the confirmed drunkard who feels himself, slowly but surely, slipping down to that awful abyss, the drunkard's hell, a foretaste of which he already feels in his soul. I have passed through it all. 'A pen of iron with the point of a diamond,' even in the hand of a Prophet Jeremiah could not describe it. Through the craving for drink and under the hellish influence of its promptings, a man will wreck his home, will lie to and deceive his best friends, his wife, and everybody who knows or trusts him.

"I had lied, stolen, and forged checks. The law, relentless as a bloodhound, urged on by outraged and defrauded creditors, was on my track. So weak I could scarcely stand or think, unable to sleep or eat, still I knew that if I did not make certain crooked things straight at once I would be arrested and locked in a felon's cell. I could see only one thing to do—just what the devil wanted me to do—and that was to go and perpetrate some crime greater than anything I had ever done. Then, in the agony of my soul, delirium tremens came upon me, as stealthily as a snake from behind my door or through the window, in the room where I vainly hoped I might get a few hours' sleep. Fiends of the most hellish forms gathered around me, holding their mouths so close that I could feel their scorching breath, telling me what to do; while my faithful, loving wife was holding me in her arms, I feared she would be frightened out of her senses by their evil plottings. The advice of these demons, whether real or imaginary, always tended towards self-destruction. Then they would go into the next room and speak so loud that I could hear every word. Often I would rise from my bed determined to end my life.

"One particular night, at Taylor's Hotel, Jersey

City, N. J., where I lived for several years, I went to the window several times, determined to end it all, but an unseen hand restrained me.

" I could mention in detail the many positions I held, procured chiefly through my brother, who though a heavy drinker himself at that time, had not been conquered by it; but I have spoken of failures enough.

"On Tuesday evening, April 18, 1882, I sat in Kirker's saloon, in Harlem, at One Hundred and Twenty-fifth Street and Third Avenue. Our home was destroyed, and my faithful, loving wife had gone back South where I had married her. She had stood by me to the last. How she could do it I cannot understand. Dear, faithful, truthful wife! She is still living, and I pray may be spared many years to me. I think I had never given her a cross word—surely she had not given me one; but our home was a drunkard's home, and all was gone. I had pawned everything or sold everything that would buy a drink. I could not sleep a wink. I had not eaten for days, and for the four nights preceding I had suffered with delirium tremens from midnight until morning.

" I had often said I would never be a tramp, I would never be cornered, for if ever that time came, I had determined to find a home in the bottom of the river. But our Lord so ordered it that when that time did come I was not able to walk one-quarter of the way to the river.

" I was sitting on a whiskey barrel for perhaps two hours, when all of a sudden I seemed to feel some great and mighty presence. I did not know then what it was. I learned afterwards that it was Jesus, the sinner's Friend. Dear reader, never until my dying day will I forget the sight presented to my horrified gaze. My sins appeared to creep along the wall in letters of fire. I turned and looked in another direction, and there I saw them again.

" I have always believed I got a view of eternity right there in that gin-mill. I believe I saw what every poor lost sinner will see when he stands unrepentant and unforgiven at the bar of God. It filled me with an unspeakable terror. I supposed I was dying and this was a premonition. I believe others in the saloon thought I was dying, but I cared very little then what people thought of me. I got down from the whiskey barrel with but one desire, and that was to get away from the place.

" A saloon is an awful place to die in if one has had a praying mother. I walked up to the bar and pounded it with my fist until I made the glasses rattle. Those near by who were drinking looked on with scornful curiosity. I said:

" ' Boys, listen to me; I am dying, but I will die in the street before I will ever take another drink '—and I felt as though this would happen before morning.

" A voice said to me: ' If you want to keep that promise, go and have yourself locked up.' There was no place on earth I dreaded more than a police station, for I was living in daily dread of arrest; but I went to the police station in East One Hundred and Twenty-sixth Street, near Lexington Avenue, and asked the captain to lock me up.

" ' Why do you want to be locked up?' asked he as I gave an assumed name.

" ' Because,' said I, ' I want to be placed somewhere so I can die before I can get another drink of whiskey.'

They locked me up in a narrow cell, No. 10, in the back corridor. That has become a famous cell to me since. For twenty years I have visited that same cell on the anniversary of that awful night of darkness, and have had sweet communion there with Jesus.

" It seemed that all the demons that could find room came in that place with me that night. They were not all the company I had either. No, praise the Lord! the dear Saviour Who came to me in the saloon was present, and said:

" ' Pray! ' I did fall on my knees on that stone floor, and said:

" ' God be merciful to me, a sinner.' As soon as I was able to leave my cell, I was taken to the police court and arraigned before Justice Bixby. He was very kind, and spoke carefully to the officer about my case, and remanded me back to the cell. When they deemed it safe to let me go, Mr. Knox McAfee, the clerk of the court, came down to my cell and let me go free. I made my way to my brother's house, where every care was given me. While lying in bed the admonishing Spirit never left me, and when I arose the following Sabbath morning I felt that that day would decide my fate.

V

MEETING JESUS

"MANY plans were turned over in my mind, but all were rejected, and towards evening, at the suggestion of a fellow-sinner, I went to the Jerry McAuley Cremorne Mission, No. 104 West Thirty-second Street. It was Sunday night, and the house was packed. With great difficulty I made my way through the crowded aisle to the space near the platform. There I saw that man of God, that apostle to the drunkard and outcast, Jerry McAuley.

" I glanced about the room and saw a mixed crowd, I assure you. It was the regular rescue mission audience that I have grown so familiar with since—pickpockets, thieves, drunkards, harlots, sporting men and women, and up near Jerry some glorious women, too. Only one glance was needed to tell me what they were doing there. They were there because it was good fishing-ground and they were helping Jerry to bring immortal souls to Jesus' feet.

" Jerry arose amid deep silence, and told his experience—that simple story I have heard so many hundred times since, but which was ever new—how he had been a ' thief, an outcast, yes, a regular bum; but,' he would add, ' I gave my heart to God, and He saved me from whiskey and tobacco and everything that's wicked and bad. I used to be one of the worst drunkards in the Fourth Ward, but Jesus came into my heart and took the whole thing out of me, and I don't want it any more.'

"I never heard this kind of Gospel before, with all the sermons I had heard, and I began to say to myself: 'I wonder if I, too, could be saved?' There was a sincerity about this man's testimony that carried conviction with it. I listened to the testimony of probably twenty-five redeemed drunkards, every one of whom told my story. They had all been saved from rum. When the invitation was given, I raised my hand and soon was kneeling down with quite a crowd of drunkards.

"Reader, how I wish I could bring that scene before you. Never till my dying day will I forget it. How I wondered if I could be saved; if God would hear me. I was a total stranger, but I felt that I had sympathy, and it helped me.

"Jerry made the first prayer. I shall never forget it.

"'Dear Saviour, won't You look down in pity upon these poor souls? They need Your help, Lord; they cannot get along without it. Blessed Jesus, these poor sinners have got themselves into a bad hole. Won't You help them out? Speak to them, Lord; do, for Jesus' sake. Amen.'

"Then Mrs. McAuley prayed fervently for us.

"'Dear Saviour,' she said in closing, 'I was a drunkard down in Cherry Hill fourteen years ago, and You saved me. Save these poor drunkards, for Jesus' sake.'

"Then Jerry sang in his peculiar voice, still kneeling:

> "'There is a fountain filled with blood,
>   Drawn from Immanuel's veins;
> And sinners plunged beneath that flood
>   Lose all their guilty stains.'

I had heard that dear old song years before around our fireside at evening prayer, in my happy childhood, and it came back like a sweet memory.

"' Now, all keep on your knees and keep praying,' said Jerry, 'while I ask these dear souls to pray for themselves.' He spoke to one and another as he placed his hand upon their heads, saying: ' Brother, pray. Now, tell the Lord what you want Him to do for you.' How I trembled as he approached me. Though I had knelt down with the determination to give my heart to God, when it came to the very moment of decision I felt like backing out. The devil knelt beside me and whispered crimes in my ears that I had forgotten for months. I had standing against me at that moment one hundred and twenty-five forgeries on one man alone. In the agony I had been in through drink, I had forgotten it until the devil reminded me of it there.

"' What are you going to do about these matters if you are going to be a Christian? You can't afford to make a mistake. Had you not better wait and fix these matters up and get out of some of these troubles, and then make a start? How can you go to Sing Sing prison and be a Christian?' Oh, what a conflict was going on for my poor soul.

" A blessed whisper said: ' Come.'

" The devil said: ' Be careful.'

" Jerry's hand was on my head. He said: ' Brother, pray!'

" ' I can't pray. Won't you pray for me?'

" ' All the prayers in the world won't save you unless you pray for yourself.' I halted but a moment,
and then with a breaking heart I said:

" ' Dear Jesus, can You help me?'

" Dear reader, never with mortal tongue can I
describe that moment. Although up to that time my
soul had been filled with indescribable gloom, I felt
the glorious brightness of the noonday sunshine in
my heart. I felt that I was a free man. Oh, the
precious feeling of safety, of freedom, of resting on
Jesus. I felt that Christ with all His love and power
had come into my life.

> " ' Sinking and panting as for breath,
>   I knew not that help was near.
> I cried: " Oh, save me, Lord, from death,
>   Immortal Jesus, hear me."
> Then quick as thought I felt Him nigh;
>   My Saviour stood before me;
> I saw His brightness around me shine,
>   And shouted, " Glory, Glory." '

And I have been shouting ' Glory ' pretty much all the
time since. From that moment until now I have never
wanted a drink of whiskey, and have never seen money
enough to make me take one. The precious touch of
Jesus' cleansing blood in my soul took from my
stomach, my brain, my blood, and my imagination, the
hell-born desire for whiskey.

" Hallelujah! What a Saviour!

" I promised God that if He would take me from
the bondage of strong drink, I would work for Him
the rest of my life. He has done His part, and I am
trying to do mine.

" One other thing has never ceased to be a wonder: I was so addicted to profanity that I would swear in my sleep. I could not speak ten consecutive words without an oath. The form or thought of an oath has never presented itself to me since. Bless His dear name forever.

" A few weeks afterwards the dear Lord showed me I was leaning on tobacco, and that I had better lean entirely on Him. I threw my plug away one night down the aisle of the Mission, and the desire was removed; in fact, tobacco was the only real sacrifice I ever made for Jesus, for I would gladly have paid money if I had it, to be freed from rum!

" The wonderful mystery of God's love for sinners never ceased to excite the most lively emotions in my breast, and has never become an old story. How the precious, pure, and spotless Saviour could stoop down and bear away my drunkenness and delirium tremens, to this day fills my soul with the tenderest gratitude.

" Surely, 'if any man be in Jesus Christ, he is a new creation.'

" How are you going to explain the physiological conditions of a man's stomach and brain, when but a moment before he would almost commit murder for a glass of rum, and after the precious blood has touched his soul he abhors it? It is simply the Divine, miraculous power of Jesus casting out demons as He did when on earth. ' Jesus Christ, the same yesterday, to-day, and forever.' (Heb. xiii. 8.)

" Oh, sinner, are you reading these lines? Before you close this book, take Him to your heart, and life, and death can never part you.

"When I arose from my knees in the Cremorne Mission after this glorious vision filled my soul, I related my experience, and for the first time told the truth—mind you, the truth so far as I remember it. All drunkards are liars, and my candid opinion is, that it is the last thing that any person is saved from.

"People crowded around me and shook hands with me. I was amazed. I didn't know what to make of it. I had not shaken hands with anyone for six months except some barkeeper whom I wanted to ' hang up' for a drink.

"I made friends that night that have stood by me ever since. Yes, I got acquainted with some of the aristocracy of heaven that night. I went out in the street and looked up to the sky. I don't believe I had looked up for ten years. A drunkard never looks up —he always looks down. It was a glorious starlight night, and it seemed to me that I could see Jesus looking at me out of a million eyes.

"'Dear Jesus,' I cried, ' You know You have saved me. But how am I going to stay saved?' Already the devil had thrown a shadow across my path:

"'You are saved; of course you are; but you'll fall, and you'll be awful sorry for all the fuss you have made to-night.' It seemed to me that Jesus said so plainly:

"'My child, work for Me. There are thousands who would come to Me if they only knew Me. Go and tell them.'"

What S. H. Hadley heard Jesus say to him so plainly was ever the inspiration of his life. I have never met one who was so evidently desirous of doing the will of God as he, but while he delighted to serve all classes of people and was willing to give heed to the most ordinary invitation for service, yet whenever there was brought to his attention a poor lost drunkard he was entirely forgetful of himself, and of the weakness of his body, and I have seen him work for hours with one person alone or travel hundreds of miles if only he might help to lift some mother's burden or comfort some heartbroken wife whose loved ones had been slain by their appetite or passion for strong drink.

He was untiring in his efforts to help others. He was never too weary to go out for the lowest. He came one day to my house in the country, utterly worn out from his city work, and was told that there was a man in the county jail who had committed a crime under the influence of drink. Nothing would do but that he must be driven to the county seat at once, and weary as he was, he spent almost the entire afternoon labouring with the man, who, like himself, had been slain by this powerful enemy. In the edition of *Perpetual Revival,* under date of March 3d, he uses the following illustration, which greatly influenced his Christian life:

"HELP SOMEBODY ELSE

" A traveller was crossing a mountain height alone, over almost untrodden snow. For a time he went bravely along his dreary path. But with the deepening shade and freezing blast there fell a weight upon his eyes and brain which seemed irresistible. In vain he tried to shake off that fatal heaviness. At this moment his foot struck against a heap that lay across his path.

It was not a stone, though no stone could be colder, or seem to have less life. He stooped to touch it, but found a human body buried beneath a drift of snow. The next moment the traveller, though weak himself, had taken a brother in his arms, and was chafing his hands and chest and brow, breathing upon the stiff cold lips the warm breath of a living soul, pressing the silent heart to the throbbing pulse of his own generous bosom. The effort to save another had brought back to himself life, warmth, and energy. He was a man again, and instead of dropping down in dreamless sleep to die, he set himself resolutely to save the life of a brother and thereby saved himself. Thus thousands are falling around us one by one. And shall not the sight of these arouse us? Can we sleep when the Master is calling us to labour? Can we be idle and indifferent when the cries of the perishing are sounding in our ears? Is it any wonder that Christ looks with astonishment upon every loiterer and asks: 'Why stand ye here all day idle?' Is he asking you and me this question? If so, will we enter the vineyard and work, or will we stand idle until the dark shadows of night settle down around us when no man can work? What we do, we must do quickly. What is our decision? GOD WANTS AN ANSWER."

VI

A DARK PICTURE

I FIND it exceedingly difficult to write the next chapter of this book. It has always been next to impossible to think of S. H. Hadley as ever being other than the purest, noblest, truest Christian, and yet according to his own testimony he came into the glorious light out of the blackness of despair.

I was one day in Tiffany's great jewelry establishment in New York making some inquiry about the setting of a ring, when I asked the salesman regarding some valuable pearls about which I had heard a customer at my side speaking. He courteously said to me, " I shall be glad to show them to you," and taking out a square piece of black velvet, he spread it out upon the show-case, and then laid upon the black background the most beautiful pearls I had ever seen. He told me that the price of one pearl was $15,000, and that the value of it was moderate in comparison with many other gems which they had in their possession, but with the black background the pearl was almost dazzling in its beauty.

I do not know but that the black background of such a life as that of S. H. Hadley may the more marvellously exhibit the grace of God by means of which he was saved and kept for so many years.

That he was a drunkard, all his friends know who

have heard him speak. He never forgot to tell it nor did he ever forget to couple with it the story of his salvation. I have heard the story repeated hundreds of times, but the last time it was as fresh and new as if I had never heard it before. I never heard him speak without shuddering. It seemed to me that he must be telling what was not true, and yet those who loved him through the long years of his weary wandering have also repeatedly affirmed that in his testimony the half had scarcely been told.

That he was guilty of forgery we know from his testimony. One hundred and twenty-five forgeries were committed against one man alone, but then as he has frequently said, " If a man is a drunkard all other sins follow in the wake of drunkenness."

He has also told us himself that he was not truthful. In his early days he represented to those who did not know him that he was a lame soldier and that his lameness came about as a result of the battle at Stone River. Frequently there were unscrupulous lawyers who wanted to secure him a pension, and once or twice when not quite himself he was almost on the point of yielding to their solicitations. His own wife did not know that the story was not true. His beloved brother and his wife knew, however, and when he professed conversion Colonel Hadley said to his wife, " I can soon tell you whether Hopkins is converted or not." When under the influence of the Spirit of God he had made the wrong right with his true and noble wife and the wife of his brother, as the Colonel entered his home one evening his wife told him that she was sure that Hopkins had been converted. " Did he tell his wife that lie? " said her husband. " Yes," said she,

" he did." Colonel Hadley began to tremble, immediately left the room, was powerfully impressed and confessed afterwards that if his brother had failed to make that wrong right he would never have believed in him, but because of his honest confession he knew that the story of his conversion must be true.

He was also a gambler. I feel a sense of heart-sickness as I record the words, but the story is from his own lips and one of his escapades is described by himself as follows:

" A Fourth of July celebration in the year 1865 was going on at Logan, Ohio, and I went down with a delegation from Straitsville to celebrate. I was a reckless, drinking gambler.

" My girl was among a waggon-load dressed in stars and stripes. They were as pretty a lot of country girls as Salt Lick Township could turn out. It was in the year 1865. The war was just over and the war feeling was very strong.

" All the local big-bugs rolled off yards and yards of patriotism on the grandstand of the Hocking County race-track down in Logan that day where the crowds gathered to hear them, as well as to see the waggon-loads of pretty girls and mingle with the thousands who were filled with patriotism, importance, and fighting whiskey. There was many a fight there that day.

" About two o'clock, while old Tom Millard was spouting patriotism from the speaker's stand to the eager crowd of listeners, Dan Kline from Lancaster came to me and said:

" ' I've been hunting for you, Hopp. Let's go up to Abe Spencer's saloon and have a little game.'

" ' I'm in,' said I, ' only I must go and tell my girl.
I came down here with Phebe,—and you know her
father is a preacher, and he didn't want to let her come,
but I told him I would take extra good care of her.'

" And so I went and told her to go straight to the
American House as soon as the speaking was over,
and to wait until I came. She said, ' All right; don't
stay long,' and I said, ' No, honey,' for we liked each
other right well.

" When we got to Spencer's, we all took another
round of drinks and then began a seven-up game, such
as you never saw. Old Rudy Duvall was my partner,
and Noel Starring sat opposite Kline. We played
four-handed for several hours, when Noel said he must
quit and go home with his wife, or she would go
crazy. Since Starring was a loser we let him go.
It was a rule in the game in Ohio that so long as the
loser has a cent left he has the right to keep the game
going, though he may stop whenever he pleases as
long as he is the loser; but the winner can never jump
the game.

" When Noel had gone, Dan says to me:

" ' Hopp, I'll play you a single-handed at two dollars
a game.'

" ' Make it three,' said I, and he agreed, so at it
we went. I had about sixty dollars in my pocket and
old Rudy had a pocketful of bills and plenty in the
bank, and he swore he'd back me for a long game with
every dollar he had or could get. We became deeply
interested; as we played, I warmed to the game but
lost right along. Dan kept cool and won every time.
It made me mad to see how cool Dan kept. During
the game he would smile and sing snatches of a cam-

paign song that I had never heard,—a line at a time, and I really believe it was the attention I paid to that song that made me lose. It ran like this:

" ' O where, tell me where was old Abraham Lincoln born?
    O where, tell me where was old Abraham Lincoln born?
    In an old Kentucky cabin one cheerless winter morn;
    In the Hardin County hills, he was raised to plow the corn.

" ' O, who led the Yeomanry in battle, tell me who?
    O, who led the Yeomanry in battle, tell me who?
    It was Honest Abe, my boy, who stands at six feet two,
    A stalwart, gallant warrior, to battle for the true.'

" My last dollar was gone and I stirred up old Rudy, who was asleep under a table, and he loaned me a hundred. We sent for some supper and played while we ate, while a big crowd of countrymen looked on. It seemed as though my luck would never turn. We changed the deck of cards for a new deck at my demand, but yet I lost and lost until my borrowed hundred dollars was gone with the rest, and old Rudy Duvall was broke as well as myself. The sun was rising, for we had played all night. And since the old man under the table was dead drunk and I was dead broke, I put up my horse against a hundred dollars and played Dan ' two best out of three.' We had won game about and stood six to six. Dan handled the cards and turned a Jack, which gave him the game and my horse. Then I put up the horse that my girl had ridden to town, and staked him against the critter that Dan won. This time we played ' three best out of five.' Again Dan's luck stayed by him and I had nary a horse left. Then I played the saddles and bridles. I couldn't win anything; but that old song kept running through my muddled brains:

" 'O where, tell me where was old Abraham Lincoln born?
In the Hardin County hills where he used to plow the corn,
In an old Kentucky cabin one cheerless winter morn.'

" I cussed Dan and cussed old Abe and his cabin and his cornfield, and cussed my luck.

" Just then Phebe sent me word that she had been sitting up all night in her dress of stars and stripes, waiting to go home, asking me when I proposed to go with her. I sent her word that I was stuck in a game and would never go home unless my luck turned. Dan said he was ready to stop any time. Of course he was; and unless I could raise a stake I could not prevent him from stopping with all my money and property in his possession.

" I reached down under the table and took the watch out of old Duvall's pocket as he snored in a drunken sleep, and played the watch against fifty dollars. Would you believe it? I lost it! It went with the rest. Then Dan looked at me kind of sheepish and said:

" 'What's the matter with playing your own watch?'

" It was a watch that my brother Harry had won in the army and had sent to me from the South. He won it at a shooting match. Sixty-two men had put up two dollars apiece to buy the watch and then shot for it. He won it, and sent it to me for safe keeping. I told him that it was my brother's watch, but I could not raise another 'ante' so up it went, to be lost like the rest.

" ' I really pity you,' said Dan, ' I thought you could play cards.'

" I looked at him a minute, then with a kick roused old Duvall and told him to go to the bank and get some money. It was now ten o'clock Thursday morning. He went willingly, saying that he would break the bank if necessary. He could borrow all he wanted.

" While old Rudy Duvall was gone for the money, I took out my revolver, the only piece of property that I had left, and laid it upon the table, saying:

" ' I'll play you this against ten dollars.'

" ' No, sir!' said Dan, rising. ' I've given you every chance, but I've sworn that I'll never play against a revolver. It means bad luck.'

" ' You'll play against it or I'll play against you!' said I, in half-drunken desperation.

" Dan looked troubled and mad. We neither of us had had a wink of sleep and not much to eat, and the rum was telling on us fearfully.

" Finally Dan tossed a whiskey-soaked bill on the table and we cut for deal. I won and turned a Jack. Then I made High, Low and the Game, which put my score four to his nothing. I held the ace and the deuce and won the game, which put me out—seven to his nothing. Then I played the revolver and the bill against twenty dollars and won. Then I played the whole ' pot ' against forty dollars and won again. My luck had changed.

" We stopped to eat dinner, which was sent in to us, and old Rudy came in with five hundred dollars that he had borrowed at the bank, but I didn't need it.

" After dinner we played all day, all that night and all day Friday and Friday night, and all day Saturday.

"Dan was worn out and demoralised. I had won back all my property, all of the money that I had lost, and during Saturday night and Sunday forenoon I got four hundred and eighty dollars of Dan's cash— all he had. He wasn't singing any more or smiling, and apparently didn't care whether Honest Abe was born in Hardin County or in Perry County, and he didn't give a cent who led the Yeomanry. We were a sorry looking pair! Dan's eyes were away back in his head, and mine looked like holes burnt in a blanket. I offered to lend him some money to go home with, but he swore he would walk, and didn't take a cent.

"The landlady loaned my girl a hat and skirt, and she jumped upon the saddle as fresh as a rose, though I could see that she had been crying.

"'Oh, what will Pap say?' was all that Phebe said.

"My! but the horses were fresh and they laid as straight as foxes all the way home—sixteen miles.

"When we reached Phebe's home I hitched the horses near the door and while Phebe went timidly in I hesitated. Her father came out looking mad and worried, and said:

"'You needn't have hitched. You can't come in here!'

"But I walked up to the old man, took his hand and asked him not to condemn me unheard. He listened while I related the whole story just as it happened. When I came to the part where I began to win, he seemed much interested, and when I said that I had won all of Dan Kline's four hundred and eighty dollars, he looked me in the face eagerly and said:

"'Did you get the money?'

" In reply, I pulled out wads and rolls and handfuls of small bills, and the old man's eyes bulged out.

" ' Come right in,' he said, ' it's near bedtime; turn in and have a good sleep. You need it.'

" We had corn bread and coffee for supper—I never tasted anything so good before.

" The money did me no good; I never won a dollar that stayed by me and I aged five years that one night."

This is in part the story of the sad, sad career of this noble man of God. Grace, it would seem to me, never did a more perfect work than in his salvation. I have known him intimately for years. I have never in all my life known one who was so pure, so true, and so Christlike in all his dealings and experiences with his fellow men, as S. H. Hadley. He was saved through and through, he was literally made over by the power of God and what God did for him he can do for anyone who will trust Him.

The fascination of gambling is something awful, and from this sin S. H. Hadley was completely delivered— he hated cards ever after the day he was saved.

There is really no sin from which Christ cannot completely deliver.

VII

OUR FIRST MEETING AND OUR LAST

MORE than fifteen years ago I was holding a series of meetings in Jersey City, N. J., and when a mutual friend said to me, "How would you like to see the slums of New York?" I answered: "I should be delighted if we could make the journey under the direction of someone who would go with us, not as a matter of curiosity, but with a desire to help the helpless," and my friend, the Rev. B. Fay Mills, said: "I will ask S. H. Hadley to go with us." I had heard his name often before this, but did not know him,—in fact I knew little about rescue mission work, and almost nothing about Water Street, except that I had heard, of course, of Jerry McAuley. At 11 P. M. we crossed the ferry and came into the city of New York. On a street corner in the lower part of the city, which was then overrun with iniquity, I first saw S. H. Hadley. He was standing underneath an old-fashioned gas lamp, and his first question addressed to us was: "Where do you want to go,— what do you want to see,—why are you here?" Mr. Mills said: "We want to go through the slums; we would like to see the effects of sin upon a human life, —my friend and I only want to go that we may cry out the more vehemently against sin, and work the more faithfully to reclaim the lost." We visited the lodging house in which he was then interested, and I was perfectly amazed to see that he had no words but those of kindness for everyone. There were drunken, swearing men about him, but his words were only words of gentleness and love. We made our way to a low-down dance hall, and when the man who was playing at the piano stopped, Mr. Hadley began to sing, " Do you know why I love Jesus." Everyone listened to him,—most of those present cried with him, and when the song was over he said: " Boys, I was once a drunkard myself, and Jesus saved me. If you ever want a friend, come to Water Street." We made our way into one of the lowest sub-cellars which existed in New York before the Parkhurst crusade. Cursing men and women were on every side of us, some were sleeping, others gambling, some were fighting,—the confusion was awful. When Mr. L. B. Greenwood, who was of our party, began to sing, " I was once far away from the Saviour, and as vile as a sinner could be," the shouting ceased, the cursing was hushed, a holy calm settled upon the company and then S. H. Hadley gave his invitation, " Come to Water Street, men and women, and you will always find a friend."

We made our way into a house of shame, and here Mr. Hadley dropped upon one knee and began to pray. His prayer was to the Saviour who had saved him when he was no better than the women before him, and he begged Him to open their eyes to their sad condition, and to save them as He had saved him. He had not uttered half a dozen sentences when the secret of his power was revealed. Every word came straight from his heart with a burning force which seemed to sweep everything before him. Those who heard him knew he meant every word of it. The women gazed at him with wide open, wondering eyes, for now he was praying for them, and as they listened a softened expression crept over their faces, and the eyes of one young girl in particular drooped and filled with tears. When he raised from the attitude of prayer, he gently put his hand upon her shoulder and said: " My sister, this is an awful life; Jesus saved me from it, and He will save you. Do come to Water Street if you need a friend. Good-bye to you all,"—and as we passed out of the house the madam who kept it said: " Thank you, sir, you are very good to come and help us." It was by this time two o'clock in the morning, and as we said good-bye it was then that he turned his face and looking full into mine, said: " Oh! Oh! Oh!! if we could only save these poor people whom Jesus loves! My brother, never preach anything but the gospel, and a gospel to save such poor lost men and women as we have seen to-night. Good-night,"— and he limped away in the darkness, leaving us with tear-wet cheeks and hearts burning with a passion to preach the gospel.

He came to the Pacific coast when we were in the midst of an evangelistic campaign there. Concerning this visit he writes as follows in his last report:

" My own health has been miserable. Last winter I feared I would break down, but just in the nick of time, Mr. John S. Huyler invited me to go with some friends in his private car to the Pacific coast and back. Just think of it, dear reader, an old drunkard, such as I used to be, who would have been glad in the old life to beat it on a freight car, or as the boys call it, in a side-door Pullman, to be invited by one of the noblest men in this country to make a trip for six

weeks in his private car, and not cost me a cent!
'And no good thing will He withhold from those who
walk uprightly.' Mr. Huyler is our greatest friend and
stands by us like a rock. Many a drunkard has he
brought here who has found salvation."

I sent him word to come to Oakland for a midnight
theatre meeting. He was too lame to walk, of course,
and so the committee provided him with a carriage.
He headed the midnight procession, and when I entered the opera house I found that he had slipped in
by the stage door and was ready to speak. He was at
his best, although suffering from weakness. He made
his appeal and sat down. I felt that possibly someone
else might come if I asked them to do so and arose to
speak, when I noticed a man of rather distinguished
appearance standing on the stage. I beckoned him to
take my unoccupied chair while I made the appeal. I
had just begun to speak when I overheard the following conversation:

"Mr. Hadley, I guess you don't know me, but you
know my brothers and my mother. They live in the
city of D——, and my name is K——." I stopped a
moment, and I heard the great rescue mission worker
say: "Are you Jimmie?" "Yes," said the man with
a sob, "I am Jimmie," and as I turned backward to
look, S. H. Hadley had his arm about his shoulder
and was saying to him, "Why, man, I know your
brothers, and your own precious mother told me you
were on this coast, and that I might find you. Why
not kneel now and let me ask God to save you?" and
while all was hushed in the audience, and every eye
riveted upon the two kneeling men, such a prayer was
poured out as only S. H. Hadley could offer. He rose

from his knees with a shout, and Jimmie, whose mother had prayed for him, and whose heart had almost broken over him, was converted. It has been said by those who knew, that when she heard of her boy's coming home, she said: "I shall now die in peace," and die she did. Her boy was thoroughly converted, so Mr. Hadley informed me, and will one day meet his mother in the skies.

The last time I saw Mr. Hadley was in Syracuse, N. Y. I had received a letter from him saying that he was coming up just for a visit, and when I was seated in a room one morning engaged in a conference, I heard him coming. I could heard the thump of his cane on the floor and his peculiar step, which was known to all who loved him. Entering the room he sat down, and the sweetest smile I have ever seen upon a man's face wreathed his as he said: "I have come up just for a few days of rest and to catch the spirit of revival," and he not only caught it, but he gave it to others. He was at his best in his speaking,— he thrilled the people with his messages, they laughed and cried and shouted as he addressed them. He expected again to go to the theatre meeting, but he said to Dr. Ostrom, who accompanied him on his last meeting: "I am tired out, and so if you will say good-bye to the people, I will get into the carriage and go to the train. God bless you, dear brother," said he, and was gone.

VIII

HIS LAST DAYS

RETURNING from Syracuse, he made his way to Stamford, Conn., to be the guest of his beloved friend, Mr. Walter M. Smith, one of New York city's prominent business men, for years a trustee at Water Street, and one of the noblest of men. S. H. Hadley loved him. The fellowship of these two chosen servants of Christ was beautiful,—never more so than the Sunday they spent together, his last but one upon the earth.

Sunday afternoon he made an impassioned appeal to the men, speaking with greater force than ever. Sunday evening he addressed the young people in the First Presbyterian Church, Stamford, Conn., and it was most fitting that the last public service he should hold in a church should be in the church of Dr. Ottman, who had known and loved him for years. From Stamford he returned to New York early Monday morning. At the station he met a man whom he had known in other days, and realising that he was hungry, in a way that was peculiarly his own, he provided food for the one who was in need of it, and then entering a carriage he made his way to a florist's. The daughter of W. M. Smith, whose guest he was over Sunday, was just recovering from an operation and was still in a New York city hospital. Purchasing the flowers he made his way to this hospital. He was not willing that an attendant should carry his offering to the suffering one, but made his way into her presence, placing the floral offering before her, with words of cheer and his bright happy smile which always made everybody feel the stronger; then he set his face towards the old Mission. He took lunch at the Mission; from one to four, as was his custom, he received those who desired to see him. Then hearing that in Bellevue Hospital one of the men who had fallen away was just recovering from an attack of delirium tremens, he entered his carriage, and taking with him one of the mission converts, who had not been as kind to the suffering one as he should have been, he made his way to the hospital, which was the scene of so many of his acts of kindness, and speaking kindly to the one in distress and offering up a prayer for his deliverance, he again went back to old Water Street.

Strangely enough, feeling stronger than usual, that night because there was no leader present, he himself conducted his last Water Street meeting. He spoke on the fifth chapter of Matthew. There were several backsliders present, and he dwelt particularly on the love and mercy of God to such. He tried to encourage them to take a new stand and to trust in God's forgiveness.

While he was dressing on Tuesday morning, he was suddenly taken ill. The old pain which had so frequently distressed him, and for which he had before spent much time in the hospital, came upon him with renewed force. He sent for a physician, who stayed with him through the morning hours and gave him some massage treatment, but the pain steadily increased. He took no luncheon, but later on in the day made his way to the office of Mr. Walter M. Smith, and said to Mr. Smith and to his partner, Mr. Cutter, "I've come to ask you to help me; I want your annual subscription, and I won't ask you for any more this year." This was his last appeal for Water Street from any source. The money was given, and this is the final entry on the books of the Mission of his personal collections. How true his message was, that this was the last appeal he would make!

On his way to Mr. Smith's office he had stopped at the Southern Railroad office, and had purchased tickets for himself and wife, expecting in a few days to go South. In this Southern trip he was to join me in Dallas, Texas, and I can see him now as he said: "If you will just give me a chance with the drunkards of Dallas, I shall be perfectly happy; it won't tire me, and it will be a real old-fashioned vacation."

At five o'clock, feeling that he was growing worse each moment, he telephoned for Mrs. Carrie Besserer, who had for so many years been the object of his special interest, and not only his, but of Mrs. Hadley's. She was counted by them both as their adopted daughter. Mr. Hadley asked her by telephone to come to him quickly. She was in the Tombs on mission work, but came hurriedly and to her he said: "I am going to the hospital, but do not say anything about it." He then went alone up to the room of Mrs. Hadley and said: "Lizzie, I am not well; I am going up to the hospital and may be gone all night, but I will be back in the morning." He put his bedroom slippers in his pocket and kissing her good-bye made his way down the stairs. On his way he met the cook, Mr. William Quinn, and said also to him: "I am going up to the hospital, but I think I shall be back to-morrow; good-bye,—God bless you." " Are you worse, Mr. Hadley? " said Quinn, and he hurriedly called Mrs. Lamont, the faithful missionary. She came and Mr. Hadley said again: " Do not say anything about this to anyone. Good-bye and God bless you." He limped his way down the stairs with Mrs. Besserer to the carriage that was waiting for them. Five men were standing out-side the Mission, and the last bit of mission work he did was to give help to three of them, and then say to the other two: " Boys, you mustn't stand around like this, go out and try to do something for Jesus."

He soon reached the hospital, where he was given, not only because of his prominence in Christian work, but because of what he was in himself, the very best of treatment. Mr. John S. Huyler and Mr. Walter M. Smith, his devoted friends, were summoned to his side, and spent the day with him. They earnestly advised him to accept the diagnosis of the surgeons and abide its consequences. The case was diagnosed and an operation seemed imperative. Mr. Hadley was unwilling to take an anæsthetic, because he knew the weakness of his heart, but when his true friends by his side urged him to submit to the doctor's suggestion, he gracefully yielded, and said: " Very well, living or dying, I am the Lord's." The operating physicians were doctors Brown and Elliott, and there also came to stand beside him and give all the help that was pos-sible Dr. Garmany, one of the most distinguished physicians not only in New York, but in the country. He counted it a privilege to give up his great work for the time and assist this poor worn-out missionary, whose joy had been to live for Christ. Strangely enough the anæsthetic did not seriously disturb his heart, but his poor body was worn out. He had literally given himself soul and body to Christ, and when the time came for recuperation there was not sufficient physical strength to withstand the awful suffering and the weakness attendant upon the operation.

Only three of his friends were with him. For three days no one was allowed to see him, but the nurse said that in his delirium he was leading the meetings in Water Street, appealing to the lost to come to Christ, and singing the hymns which were so dear to him and to all the friends of Water Street. He is credited with saying as he was nearing his end, " What will become of my poor bums? " but so far as we can find out, and after consultation with those who were with him at the last, he did not make use of this expression. He sometimes in a playful joking way spoke of the converts as " bums," and called himself a " bum," but in his serious, sober moments the converts of Water Street were the noblest men upon earth, and were always spoken of by him as such. He did manifest the deepest concern, not only for the converts of the Mission, but for those who were still unsaved, and it is true that his last breath was used to express concern for their safety and hope for their ultimate salvation.

On February 9, 1906, at 5.30 in the morning, he breathed his last. He slept his way into eternity. From 12 to 4 there was not a struggle, but sleeping sweetly as a child he went into glory. So many times in his sleep the nurse would hear him whispering, and bending over him, she would hear him say, " Precious Jesus! Precious Jesus! " When he opened his eyes that morning, it was to look into the face of Him whom not having seen, he passionately loved.

When any of his friends were permitted to see him, he never lost an opportunity to send some message to those in whom he was interested. He sent a greeting to me when he feared the end had come, in which he said: "Tell Chapman that I can do more for him at the Throne than I can do here," and I have ever since believed it. When the message was conveyed to me, I sent it on to a mutual friend, Mr. John R. Clements, of Binghamton, N. Y., and he returned it to me with the following:

> "I can do more for him yonder
> Than I could if I were here."

Walk we here in Christian service
  Hand with hand, and heart to heart;
While the love of Jesus binds us,—
  Silken cord that ne'er can part.
Reaching out to lift the fallen,
  Speaking words of help and cheer;
Striving just to do what Jesus
  Would be doing, were He here.

CHORUS:

Passing on! The workers leave us—
  But 'tis only seeming so;
Yonder at the throne eternal
  They our trials and struggles know.
In the palace-halls of Heaven
  Oft they pray, our hearts to cheer:
"I can do more for him yonder,
  Than I could if I were here."

In the by-ways, 'mid the hedges,
  In the haunts of vice and sin
With a heart of tender pity
  Seeking wretched souls to win;
On the heights of worldly splendour
  'Mid its dazzle and its mirth,
Holding up " the cross of Jesus "
  Fairest spectacle of earth.

Here and there, where'er is sorrow,
  Here and there, in paths of woe,
With the words of life eternal
  E'er in eagerness to go.
In the world so much that's bitter;
  O, so much that's wicked here!
Hands grow weak; the toil is heavy;
  Dimmed the eye with many a tear.

God, O God of Battles, strengthen
  Every arm that fights in love,
Till the last soiled soul immortal
  Sights the gates of peace, above;
Then around the throne eternal,
  When the earth has passed away,
Will each servant sing of Jesus,
  Through one never-ending day.

IX

LOVE

IN the thirty-eighth chapter of Isaiah and the seventeenth verse, the following words are found, "Thou hast in love to my soul delivered it from the pit." The marginal reading is: "Thou hast loved my soul from the pit."

A better description of S. H. Hadley could not be given. He was the best exemplification of the love of Christ in his seeking after lost men and caring for them when once they were found of any person I have ever known. Again and again I have heard him say that the reason why Christians so often fail in reaching the lost is that they do not have the spirit of love. The thirteenth chapter of 1st Corinthians was his creed and he never was unfaithful to it so far as I know. Men might deceive him, but he would love them; they might disappoint him, but he would still continue to love them; indeed, the farther one seemed to be away from Christ the more he became the object of the love of this devoted servant of Jesus Christ. He once told me that if he could in any way help to stimulate this spirit throughout the Church we would have such a revival as the world had never seen.

One of the best illustrations of his spirit along this line is found in his treatment of one who was known as "Bowery Ike." The following has been written by a friend of the Water Street Mission:

"It was 'Rummy' who first called Mr. Hadley's

attention to Bowery Ike. That was in September,
1884. Ike was one of the most alert thieves in New
York. He made it his ' specialty ' to go into buildings
where carpenters were at work, and steal the watches
from their coats when these were hanging up. In
describing his prowess, Rummy said enthusiastically:
' Why, I have known him to swipe eight watches at a
time! Yesterday he got pinched. 'Twas too bad, for
he had got a number one gold ticker in his pocket he
was going away with.'

" The outcome of this was, that Mr. Hadley, ' the
friend of the wicked,' went to the Tombs next morning and persuaded the judge to give the thief only six
months on the Island. There Mr. Hadley visited the
boy many times, and began to like him very much. He
interested his wife in his newly found protegé, and she
began to pray for his redemption.

" Many people thought she might as well pray for the
moon, for Ike was a born thief. He had been arrested
many times, and often imprisoned. His only education
had been received in the New York Asylum, from
whence he escaped. He was a petty sneak-thief. It
is harder for a camel to pass through the eye of a
needle than for that kind of a thief to reform.

" When Ike was released Mr. Hadley got him work.
He did well, was trusted, and rose to a place of responsibility, where larger or smaller amounts passed
through his hands. In this place he did not steal, but
the monotony of such a life became intolerable to his
active temperament, and one day he disappeared.

" Some time passed before he came to the surface
again—as suddenly as he had vanished. He presented himself to Mr. Hadley, asked him for work, and

began at the bottom once more. At one time a business rival of Mr. Hadley hired Ike, thinking he had taken away Mr. Hadley's 'mascot.' But Ike stole his clothes, his watch, his money, and would have stolen his store if he could. Detectives were employed to hunt him down. Six months after that he came to Mr. Hadley again.

" ' Ike, why did you rob that man?' was the first question.

" ' Oh,' he said, 'I had to. He watched me.'

" A great love had sprung up in Mr. Hadley's heart for this poor criminal. He determined to save him, if love and prayer could do it.

" While serving his time for his last offence Ike promised his benefactor that he would forsake his vicious ways and lead an honest life. He kept his promise. Mr. and Mrs. Hadley had their reward, after the hopes and prayers of years.

" The redeemed thief gave convincing evidence of a changed purpose in life, and he did not withhold his public testimony. His old chums would drop into the Water Street Mission to make sure that it was Bowery Ike who spoke there, and if he had really stopped stealing. The habit of truth-telling came hard to the new convert, and when he transgressed, his deep remorse would cause him to get up in meeting and openly call himself a liar, and then to fully state the truth. But he never stole again, and his life continued clean, although his old companions not infrequently urged him to return to the excitements of his former life.

" He was finally sent to the Moody Bible School in Chicago, where he developed an unusual knowledge of the Bible. He had charge for eighteen months of an out-of-door mission in that city. Just as he was ready to return to his Water Street Mission he suddenly died of heart disease.

"Bowery Ike's conversion has been considered an unusual case. It took ten years of faithful and prayerful effort, under the most discouraging conditions, to lead this apparently hopeless thief into the higher, better life. It was as much of a miracle as the turning of water into wine, but to call it ' unusual ' is a mistake. Such miracles of transformation are going on constantly all around us. There is no life that has ever been lived, or ever will be lived, too vile to be made pure by allegiance to the divine Teacher, to whom poor Ike was led to give his love and the faithful service of a contrite heart."

Mr. Hadley was unique in his conduct of a meeting. Fortunately I am able to present in substance what he said to those who were present at the mission on two different occasions.

"Brethren, there must be a higher principle in religion than *feeling*. Just as sure as you depend on your feelings, and measure your religion by your feelings there will be trouble. Nobody can explain how it is and why it is that the devil, at times, gets such a control of our feelings. But he does and we feel sad and gloomy and unhappy in spite of ourselves, and then look out, for if you think your salvation depends on a happy state of feeling there will be trouble.

"But oh, brethren, do learn that your faith must be in Jesus and in *Him alone*. Let this be your song:

> "'I dare not trust the sweetest frame
> But wholly lean on Jesus' name.
> On Christ the solid rock I stand—
> All other ground is sinking sand.'

" Then there will be *no* trouble when the bad, gloomy feelings come, for your salvation is not *feeling,* but faith and trust in Christ and his promises. The peace and joy does come. It is a part of the Christian's life, but it is not always overflowing, and indeed while sometimes the joy can hardly be expressed and the 'peace flows like a river,' again there seems *no* peace, *no* joy, *no* light, then *trust Jesus.* Look up and say, 'Dear Jesus, thou art mine and I am thine. I trust thee to keep me in the dark and discouraging hour.

" Oh, brethren, get beyond the *fear* of falling.

" Let the thought never enter your mind. One will say, 'Now if I take that job will I keep sober? Can I stand there?' Of course you will stand if you tell everybody what you have been and what Jesus has saved you from. I have never once since the Lord saved me had one thought of taking a drink or going back into sin. But I have been careful to tell everybody what Christ has done for me. Confess Him everywhere! Oh, brethren! get on a higher plane."

In a meeting at the Mission April 24, 1896, he said: " I used to think I would be willing to crawl on my knees all my lifetime if God would keep me from wanting whiskey. But for fourteen years I have been *flying.* He don't let us crawl. Oh, dear converts, let Jesus be first and uppermost in thought and life and let all other things trail on after.

" Fourteen years this morning was my first day a Christian. I prayed at eight o'clock, 'Lord, keep me from drinking and swearing till nine o'clock.' At nine o'clock I prayed, 'Jesus, keep me from drinking and swearing till ten o'clock,' and so on all that first day, and there I learned the secret of living and walking with Jesus; trusting moment by moment. Later I learned there were other sins to be overcome besides drinking and swearing. Never have I from that day wanted or felt the *least* desire for whiskey or any sins of the old life. For three months I had a job as watchman at three dollars per week. I often thought, 'Lord, why is it I have to work for wages less than I got when a boy?' But now I look back with joy to those three months."

Another time this was a part of his testimony:

"The old ship had sunk, but there was a lot of debris floating around, old bedsteads, mattresses, chicken-coops, etc., that would not sink. I was smoking and chewing tobacco. The Lord Jesus said, 'Oh, oh, oh, my child! give it up.' I said, 'Why, Lord, it would kill me; I would surely die.'

"Jesus said, 'My child, what have you ever given up for me?' I said, 'Nothing, Lord, I never gave up anything for you, and I will give up my tobacco.' And I did it. Then the Lord showed me it was wrong to get mad and I asked him to take the mad out of me and He did that. Hallelujah, what a Saviour! Will I ever forget what Jesus has done for me?"

It is, however, the universal testimony of those who have been most faithful in their attendance at Water Street, that it was not simply Mr. Hadley's way of saying things, but what he was in himself, that counted with the men who were ready to listen to him. I once heard a man say: "Whatever S. H. Hadley may say, or however he may say it, I know he loves me because I am a lost man." In all my experience as a minister I have never known anyone, I am sure, who was so perfect an illustration of the love of Christ for sinful men as himself, and almost a countless number of people to-day rise up to call him blessed.

Mr. Hadley was an ordained Methodist minister. He had no training in the schools, but he had a great training in the school of life which so eminently qualified him for work in the Master's vineyard, so the great Methodist Church honoured herself in setting him apart in a special manner to do the work of the Master. He was ordained deacon in 1900 and set apart as a minister of the Gospel in 1904. In the *Christian Advocate* of April 21, 1904, the following reference is made to his ordination:

"A spirited but pleasant discussion took place on the question of granting local elder's orders to S. H. Hadley, the Superintendent of the Water Street Mission. New York East Conference rarely gives ordination to brethren not entering the regular ministry, but in the case of Brother Hadley, such is the interest in his work, and with such favour have his peculiar gifts been honoured, that the most careful and conservative men of the Conference gladly voted him the privileges of an elder. The speech of Professor Rice, Chairman of the Board of Examiners, in moving that Brother Hadley be elected to elder's orders was an exquisite piece of special pleading, and the same is true of that of Dr. Buckley. Dr. Downey, Dr. F. M. North, and several others added eloquent tributes to the great work Mr. Hadley is doing, and he was unanimously recommended for ordination."

Concerning this solemn service, Rev. James M. Buckley, D. D., the distinguished editor of the *Christian Advocate,* writes as follows:

"The Rev. S. H. Hadley was long a lay member of the Methodist Episcopal Church within the bounds of the New York East Conference. It is the system of the church to make use of the labours of goodly laymen having gifts, grace and usefulness, as (what are called) local preachers. The lowest grade of these is simply the right to preach and to supply pulpits at the request of pastors, or under the direction of the presiding elders. The next degree is that of a deacon; a deacon must be ordained and can baptise and assist in the administration of the Lord's Supper, and the third and last is that of elder, who can perform all the functions of a minister. A course of study is marked out for these classes or degrees respectively. Beside the study there must be the reading of several books. The ordination takes place at the session of the Annual Conference. Those who cannot pass the examinations are so reported to the Conference and usually they are not ordained. But at all times useful men sound in faith, with a fair acquaintance with doctrine and discipline, are dealt with considerately.

"When Mr. Hadley's case came up the Committee had to report him deficient in some of the studies and as not having read all the books. He did not reach the minimum mark on a scale of ten. The Conference sympathetically smiled, and one man asked if 'we were going to let down the bars, disregard our rules, etc.' This was not raised very seriously and several spoke of Mr. Hadley's work, his piety, his common sense, his soundness in the faith, and the blessing of God upon his labours, and *all,* including Professor William North Rice, the Chairman of the Committee of Examination, favoured his passage with the result

that it was unanimously voted, and he was duly ordained. The rumour that there were objections and
a great opposition overcome with much difficulty was
baseless."

I have no question at all but that in thus solemnly
setting apart S. H. Hadley to the work of the ministry,
the Methodist Church gave to the world one of her
most distinguished sons, and I am very sure that the
action must have had the approval of the great head
of the church.

X

WATER STREET MISSION

THE founder of the Water Street Mission, Jerry McAuley, was born in Ireland in 1837. He came to this country at the age of thirteen years and was brought up in the Fourth Ward by his grandmother. He soon got beyond her control and became a thief. At the age of nineteen he was sentenced to Sing Sing prison for a term of fifteen years and six months. In the Prison Chapel one Sunday morning " Awful " Gardner, a noted prize fighter and an all round ruffian whom Jerry had known prior to going to prison, was preaching. Gardner had been converted. When Jerry heard him he said, " That man is honest." He was deeply convicted of his sin and in his cell towards evening the light broke in upon him and he found Jesus, but after his testimonial, possibly because of lack of special assistance, certainly in part because of great temptation, he fell. This was repeated several times, but at last he was brought to Christ and the great Mission was established in 1872.

Concerning this Mission Dr. Arthur T. Pierson writes as follows:

" No. 316 Water Street, New York, is almost exactly underneath the western approach to the great suspension bridge which spans the East River. Any night of the year a good-sized room may there be found, full of men, who, for the most part, are obviously poor, given to drink and other vices; and

INTERIOR OF WATER STREET MISSION.

many faces bear the marks of crime. A few seem to have the black brand of Cain. The tramp and pauper, the pickpocket and river thief, the besotted sailor and highway robber, the procurer to lust and the blatant blasphemer—every class of the worst men and women find their way there, and one may there speak to from two hundred to three hundred of these victims of want, woe, and vice. On one night of the week these hundreds are freely fed with good bread and coffee, as well as with the Bread of Life. The Gospel is sung with rousing effect, brief and simple Gospel talks interspersed, and an after-meeting always follows for prayer and testimony, and hand-to-hand touch with inquirers.

"For over a quarter of a century, night after night in hot and cold weather, in wet and dry, with no dependence but faith in God, with no recompense but the wages of soul winners, his work has gone on, at times scarce surviving for want of funds and popular sympathy, yet always outliving any threatened danger of collapse, because God is behind it."

Thirty-four years ago, 316 Water Street was in the very core of the most villainous slum region in America. No man's life was safe in the vicinity after dark. Not a policeman could be induced to visit the locality unless armed to the teeth and accompanied by a brother officer. Every place that was not a saloon was a dance house, gambling den or a bagnio. A block away was Kit Burns' rat pit, where Kit's illustrious son-in-law, "Jack-the-Rat," used to bite a live rat's head off every night and pass the hat through the crowd for a collection.

Prize fights occurred nearly every night, and many

fights took place in which there was no prize save black eyes and broken bones. Assassination, robbery, suicide, lust and every form of crime known to darkness thrived like snakes in a tropical forest.

One day a missionary named Little invaded the neighbourhood and was confronted on a stairway by a drunken woman who wanted to fight. " Do you know Jesus? " asked the missionary by way of diverting the issue. " Faith, an' who is Jesus? " demanded the woman. Near by lay a bundle of rags within which was a human being. " What's that yez says? " demanded the rags, rising to their feet. The apparition was Jerry McAuley, drunkard, thug, thief, and ex-convict, who had just been pardoned out of Sing Sing, where he had been sentenced to nineteen years' imprisonment. Jerry had been converted in prison through the preaching of " Awful " Gardner, his prize-fighting pal, who had been converted before him; but Jerry had fallen back into the gutter before he had learned his first prayer.

Five times Jerry backslid to the depths, but he finally reached firm ground and began his work of helping others. His modest efforts attracted the attention of a few such men as A. S. Hatch, the banker, who gave him assistance. Shortly the old rookery at 316 Water Street was transformed from a dance house into a mission with Jerry in charge. That was the beginning of a movement that has worked miracles in the slums of the continent. The influence of the mission has been marvellous. One night old John Jaeger, a drunken Dutch anarchist, who couldn't speak English and who couldn't read any language whatever, staggered into Jerry's mission. Though he could not understand a word that was said, he was converted. Soon the anarchist opened a mission of his own. He called it the Mission of the Living Waters, and it was located at 136 Christie Street. The Mission is there yet and so is the " anarchist," now one of the best-known mission workers in New York.

One night John H. Wyburn, a young man who had seen better days, was on a frightful " tear " with one of Jerry's back-slidden converts. The convert sent Wyburn around to " strike " Superintendent Hadley for a loan of ten dollars. He did not get the ten dollars, but he " got salvation." This man Wyburn is now acting Superintendent of the Water Street Mission.

Years ago a dilapidated drunken tramp printer, wearing an old linen duster, staggered into the Mc-Auley Mission. The man was in a deplorable condition. The duster was frozen to his body. His feet were almost bare on the snow and ice. To-day that dilapidated creature is one of the most successful slum workers in Canada, and Superintendent of the Old Brewery Mission of Montreal.

Many years ago Colonel Henry H. Hadley was on one of his tremendous periodical " sprees." He had commanded a regiment in the Civil War and was a man of ability, but rum was his master. After gorging himself with fifty-two drinks in a single day, he wandered into Jerry's mission, where he was converted. To-day, the name of Henry H. Hadley is known wherever rescue missions are known.

Then there was " old John Wood," a sailor who was drummed out of the United States navy on account of chronic alcoholism. One dark night the poor sot

wound up a frightful debauch by starting down towards the East River to drown himself. He heard
the singing in " old Water Street," went in, and came
out a new man. A few years ago this John Wood,
superintendent of the mission of the Brooklyn Navy
Yard, died at his post, and is remembered as the
originator of Christian Endeavor work in the navy
of the United States.

One night many years ago, Mrs. E. M. Whittemore
and her husband, Sidney Whittemore, came down to
Water Street Mission, " just to see what was going
on." They belonged to the best society of New York
and wanted to find some new sensation. Both were
converted; and that dark night was the beginning of
the " Door of Hope," which now has rescue missions
in nearly every State in the Union, and most of the
large cities, for this same Mrs. Whittemore organised
that movement."

Out of the Water Street Mission has also grown
the rescue work which is under the direction of the
Methodist Church Extension Society in the City of
New York. This work is located on the Bowery.
The meetings were formerly conducted in what was
known as " Wesley Hall," but since Mr. Hadley's
death the name has been changed to " Hadley Hall."
The superintendent in charge is Rev. John Callahan,
a devoted friend of Mr. Hadley's and one of the truest
rescue mission workers in the world. As a matter of
fact the influence of the McAuley Mission has been
world wide.

Concerning his call to Water Street Mr. Hadley
writes as follows:

" On May 30, 1886, I took charge of the Water

MATTHEW J. GALLAGHER.

PROF. F. T. FITZGERALD.

Street Mission. Never shall I forget that day! After struggling for nearly two years after my conversion, I had finally gotten into a profitable business with an income of $2,500 a year, and with good prospects of a permanent future.

" I considered the call to the work in Water Street the most important a man could have, and my wife and I spent many days in prayer. Strange to say, we both got our answer reading the Scripture, Isaiah lviii. 3-12.

" Friends of the Mission decided to give us a great send-off. From the parlours I could look down into the room. It was filled with well-dressed people, Mr. R. Fulton Cutting presiding. When I saw the crowd I was frightened. I went into my bedroom and dropped on my knees and said:

" ' Lord, if you have really called me to this work, give me one soul.'

" How often have I thought of that prayer since. I could as well have had a score of souls. The meeting went on. At the close I gave the invitation, saying:

" ' Is there one man here who would like to come to Christ? ' One, and only one, raised his hand. The Lord did the best He could, according to my faith. He gave me the biggest bum and drunkard in the house. He sat on the last seat by the door, as he was too drunk to get any further.

" One of my friends had found him the night before in a stale beer dive in Mulberry Bend, and had asked him to come down.

" ' Give me fifteen cents and I'll come,' said he. My friend gave him the fifteen cents, and after spending it for whiskey, two drinks for five cents, and all the rest he could get, he came in very drunk. I said:

" ' If there are any needy souls, come up here.' He started, but was so drunk he fell to the floor. Ready hands helped him to the front. He was a fearful looking object, six feet four inches high, weighing 260 pounds, and had on only two garments, such as they were, an old pair of breeches tied around him with a piece of clothes line, and a jumper, both too short, there being a wide space between the two where there was nothing but the bare skin.

" The ladies gave him all the room he wanted to kneel in. My wife, Mrs. Sherwood, our missionary, and also Mrs. Stephen Merritt, who were present, knelt with him and prayed. Hundreds of times have I heard him tell the story in his broad Scotch dialect:

" ' I came in drunk and I went out sober, and the best of it is, I've been sober ever since. Whatever prayer it was I made that night I don't remember, but the Lord heard it, and the best of it is, He has answered it ever since. I was not fit to sleep in a bed that night. No lodging house would have kept me, so I went to Shinbone Alley in Bleecker Street and took the soft side of a truck. I went to work in a few days carrying a hod.'

" He was known at that time as ' Scottie the Bum.' Born in Glasgow, he was a drunkard from youth, and before he was seventeen years old he was committed to prison for drunkenness. He was sent to America, as so many drunkards are, and wandered all over the country drinking rum, walking ties when he could not ride a freight train, sinking lower and lower in the clutches of whiskey, until he was found by my friend.

He secured work at carrying a hod. He joined the Tile-layers Helpers' Union after he got work, and soon became the treasurer. He was the doorkeeper in the Central Labor Union for years on Sunday afternoons. Finally he was chosen walking delegate, and for seven years was elected every six months.

"He formed one of the Board of Walking Delegates of the Trades Union of New York. 'Big Jim,' as he came to be called in those days, helped settle some of the biggest strikes in New York City by his manly, candid truthfulness and hard Scotch common sense. He was finally elected Grand Marshal of the Labor Day Parade, and rode down Broadway on a big bay horse at the head of fifteen thousand of the best workmen in New York. He married a Christian woman from the Florence Crittenton Mission.

"Wishing to find other employment, he went to work for the City and Suburban Homes Company, and from a humble position he has, by his sterling integrity, worked his way up, until he is now one of the superintendents, having a lot of men under him and many houses to care for. He also has a home of his own."

Instead of "Scottie the Bum," or "Big Jim," he has been known and loved for years as Mr. J. C. Edwards.

Mr. Hadley was always more than generous in his appreciation of his assistants, and concerning his helpers in Water Street he gave this testimony:

"I have been unusually blessed with co-workers since I came here. Mrs. Sarah Sherwood was with us for ten years after we came to Water Street—Mother Sherwood, as we all called her. Probably this

woman has shaken hands with more drunkards than
any other woman in this city. She was of a distinguished Connecticut family. Two of her brothers have
been governors of their native State.

"The converts of the Mission who knew Mrs. Sherwood will never forget her. She helped to bear their
sorrows, and to share their joys. They all leaned on
her in time of trouble, and backsliders always found
in her a willing ear and a heart full of sympathy. At
the same time, she dug them out, and if they were
living on false hopes she was quick to detect it. No
one could more lovingly or skilfully uncover a liar
or a fraud than she could, and after doing so no one
would stand by them more lovingly and faithfully,
helping them to right the wrong. Her sweet and
gracious presence was well known in all the dens and
dives about here, and when she entered a saloon or
house of evil resort the swearing and vile talk instantly ceased and the barkeeper would not wait on
customers while the 'mission lady' was present. She
procured hundreds of dollars from the merchants in
the lower part of the city, and so amiable was her
manner that invitations were extended to her to come
again, and she was not slow to accept them.

"Mr. Franklin Smith was also with us all this time
—a tender, modest, lovable man, mighty in faith and
prayer. He never knew the evils of drink, but sympathised deeply with those who did. He died shortly
after Mrs. Sherwood.

"Mrs. Mary W. Bentley was also a missionary for
some five years. She lived here, and her love and faith
for lost men and women was boundless. I never
saw her out of patience. She was drawn to men

only because they were sinners sinking down to destruction and needed a friend. She was a great sufferer for months before her death, but always prayed for us to the last, and sent messages of love to those whom she loved and had led to Jesus.

"A book could be written of either of these devoted Christian lives. The ladies had ample means to support themselves, but chose to come here and work, because here is where the sinners come, and here is where they can be reached.

"Our present missionary, Mrs. Lida M. Lamont, our faithful and tireless friend, has been with us for over five years. My beloved wife and Mrs. Lamont are the only ladies who live in the building.

"One of my assistants for five years was Mr. Harry E. Prentice, a redeemed man from England, who about six years ago went into business life; but he still holds his connection with us, and often leads our meetings on Sunday evenings.

"Our present assistant is Mr. John H. Wyburn, who was saved in this Mission, while very drunk, many years ago. Three years of this time he was Superintendent of the Bowery Mission, and we are thankful to have him here now, and we trust that he will remain as long as we do."

Special mention should be made of another helper of Mr. Hadley's in the person of the pianist, Mr. Squires, a salesman in Tiffany's great jewelry establishment; for years there has scarcely been a mission service held that he has not presided at the piano in a masterful way.

Out from this Mission with such a leader and such a band of consecrated workers has gone a stream of influence which is as wide as the world in its sweep. S. H. Hadley may be dead, but the Scripture is absolutely true, " He being dead yet speaketh."

One of the features of Water Street Mission is the Thursday evening meeting, when there is a great feast spread for the hungry. This is made possible through the generosity of John S. Huyler, one of New York's most prominent business men, trustee of the Mission, and one of the best friends Mr. Hadley has ever had. The following description was given of the Thursday night service in one of the newspapers:

" At six o'clock the room was full and after seven there was not an empty seat. At this hour half a dozen of the leader's assistants disappeared and in a few moments re-entered, bearing aloft large wooden trays piled high with sandwiches. Two hundred pairs of eyes brightened instantly and two hundred pairs of lips grew parched with anxiety. They were the most generous sandwiches that the mind of man ever conceived. The sandwiches disappeared like dew before the morning sun. Cup after cup of the very best coffee was drained to the very dregs. The men then settled back with an air of comfort after they had picked the last crumbs from their worn knees and not a single man left the room when the leader of the meeting opened the gospel meeting. All this time an unassuming gentleman had occupied a seat among those on the platform. He it was who had provided the supper for the men, and who does it every Thursday night. His name is known the world over, but no schoolgirl, munching Huyler's chocolates and bonbons, ever enjoyed them as much as those poor men the sandwiches and coffee which his generosity had provided."

XI

FUNERALS AT WATER STREET

I WAS one day sitting with Mr. Hadley on the piazza of my home in the country. He was reading a New York paper when suddenly he said, dropping the paper in his lap, " Can I send a telegram from here quickly?" and I said, " Certainly." He wrote out his message on a piece of paper and I sent it over the telephone to the telegraph office in the nearby town. He had read in the paper the story of a poor fallen girl who had come to the end of her sad career and without friends to mourn over her or to bury her, she had been sent to the Morgue, of all the places in the world the most desolate. Tears stood in the eyes of the great soul winner as he wrote his message. It was sent to one of his assistants in New York and was to the effect that the body of the poor lost girl was to be taken from the Morgue and carried to Water Street. She was to be furnished, at the expense of Mr. Hadley, with a coffin and a shroud, and the Mission Workers were asked to gather around her poor worn out body to read God's Word, sing the hymns of the church and cry over her misspent life. This was the spirit of S. H. Hadley always.

He used frequently to make his way through the hospitals of New York City, especially in the wards where the poor and outcast were suffering, and whenever he found one who was near the end and was friendless, he left special instructions that he was to be notified when their death occurred, and they too would be carried to the Mission and given just such a burial as their own loved ones might have wished had they known that their life journey was ended.

One day in passing through a hospital the following sad experience was brought to his attention. It was, however, but one of a multitude of experiences all of which always filled his great heart with anguish; nevertheless, like his Master he went on to do the will of his Father and delighted to spend and be spent in the service of others.

"We were obliged," he said, "to go through the dead-house belonging to Bellevue Hospital a day or so ago. A friend had died in Bellevue and we were going to bring her out for burial. We noticed a party of women, three in number, who were evidently looking for a relative whom they hoped yet dreaded to find. There was no mistaking the character of the elder woman. She was over fifty, and of undoubted respectability. The other two ladies seemed to be friends, but we felt sure this was a mother seeking a child. No one else could stay so long in that dreadful house of death. She walked through the morgue and looked into the faces of all who lay there, then she walked down through the long, low, dead house which is built over the river. But little idea could be gained of this horrible task by reading this article. The attendants were very polite, and rendered all the aid in their power. One by one cloths were removed until she had looked carefully at all the faces. Was she looking for a daughter? Yes, she was. She was almost sure the woman whom she read of, who had committed suicide, was her daughter. 'There is another small room,' said the attendant; 'just stay here, madam, a moment,' and taking a man he disappeared into another building. Pretty soon they returned carrying between them a half-bent form covered with a black cloth. As soon as the cloth was removed from the face of the dead woman a shriek went up that the writer will remember to his dying day. 'Oh, Mary! Mary!' said the poor heart-broken mother, 'is it thus I meet you? Oh, my God, I can't bear this. Oh, Mary, Mary, is it possible this is you!' And so she went on; and with a bursting heart she tried to throw herself on the slab which held the lifeless, though disfigured body of her lost, wayward girl. The story was soon learned. It could almost be told in one word, RUM. Some devil in human shape had taught her to drink, then ruin and disgrace followed. Then despair and death closed the scene. We would prefer, though, to take our chances as Mary before the great Judge, a thousand times, than the wretch who sold her the liquor."

Experiences like this were common with this dear servant of Christ.

There have been some notable funerals at Water Street; possibly one of the most striking was held in 1892.

BILLY KELLY'S FUNERAL

In the big room of the Jerry McAuley Mission at 316 Water Street there lay in state the body of Billy Kelly, gambler, faro dealer, barkeeper, drunkard, and all-around sport, reformed a year before his death and become one of the most respected members of the mission.

The hard wooden benches in the little building were crowded with reformed outcasts and outcasts beyond all hope of reform. On one side of the coffin sat Billy's three children, Florence, Tiny, and William, Jr. On the other side were some of Kelly's old companions, among them the gambler Tom Jolly, with his wife and Mr. and Mrs. "The" Allen.

More than once during the brief and simple ceremony the famous dive keeper furtively wiped his eyes and coughed with suspicious huskiness. About the coffin were wreaths of white and pink roses, while on it lay a great mass of white lilies.

On the coffin plate was inscribed the name of William Kelly, with the date of his death on April 9, 1892, at the age of forty-seven years.

After Mr. Hadley had announced that the funeral procession would start from the Mission at 12 o'clock noon, and the interment would be in Long Island City, he asked for remarks from those who were friends of the dead man. "Let's hear from the Captain," suggested someone, and in response a short, thick-set man, whose sunburned face terminated in a bristly grey beard, arose in his place, and spoke:

"I remember well the night Billy Kelly first came in here fourteen months ago," he said, in a voice that trembled slightly. "I had just got into port from a long voyage and had come into the dear old Mission. Billy came stumbling in, a terrible wreck of what must have been a fine-looking man. I could see that he was on the edge of delirium tremens. He asked if he could get some soup there. I told him that he could after the services. 'I'm hungry,' he says, 'and I haven't a cent. For the last week I've been in hell.

Some don't believe in hell, but I've been there, been there with the drink on me, so that when I closed my eyes all the torture of a man dead and damned was in me. God help me! I don't dare sleep for fear of what comes on me when I'm asleep. It's three days now since my eyes were closed.'

" ' God help you,' says I. ' Pray to Him.' He went forward to the front, and I'll never forget the look on his face when he kneeled. ' Oh, God!' he says, ' give me sleep, sleep, only sleep and rest from the hell that's in me.' We all prayed for him, and that night he slept. After that he gave up the drink, and was one of us until death."

There were other remarks from members of the mission, showing how the dead man had been loved by all his comrades, and at the end Jim Dixon, a reformed sport and gambler, got up on his feet.

" You all knew Billy when he was in the mission," he said. " You know how good a man he was when he was reformed. But I knew the good that was in him when he was at his worst. Man and boy, for twenty odd years, I've lived with him, eaten with him, drank and gambled and starved with him. He was my partner through thick and thin, and all of you who've been gamblers and drunkards and lived up and down by your wits know what that means. I've seen him when he was in luck with five thousand dollars in his pocket, and the next week he was in Bellevue with the blue devils at his throat. When he got out he pawned his shoes and shirt for money to buy a drink, and one night when he was down to his last two dimes I saw him give away half what he had to a girl he used to know who was without money. Billy would have gone without dinner or bed that night if I hadn't found him. That's the kind of a man he was, ready always to share up with anyone worse off than himself. When he joined the Mission I'd been in hard luck, but had just struck a job dealing faro. I used to go and see him, but he wouldn't drink with me. Finally I asked him what was up with him, and he said, ' Jim, I've joined the Mission, and I'm a better man for it. I want you to come in too.' Well, I thought about it and six months ago I joined. That's one of the many things that Billy did for me. But what I remember in him is that when he was in the Mission and I was still a gambler and drinker, he never went back on me. Billy and I were partners to the end."

After the speaking was over some hymns were sung and the meeting broke up. " The " Allen, who had declined to speak in the meeting, was walking out when he caught sight of " Tiny " Kelly, the dead man's thirteen-year-old daughter. The ex-dive keeper walked up and put his hand, which trembled slightly, on the girl's shoulder.

" My child," he said, " your father was a man to remember. It took better than me to save him from himself, but if I couldn't do for him, perhaps I can do for his children. If ever you are in need, you or your brother or sister, come to me. While I have anything Billy Kelly's children can call on me.

" Billy Kelly," continued " The " Allen, turning to the crowd which had collected, " was one of the few men I knew that I could trust. My life hasn't made me trustful of men. For four years I haven't walked a block in the street in company with any man. I go my way alone, and other men can go theirs. But I didn't feel so towards Billy. I knew the house where he was born down on Carmine street, near Bleecker. I knew the boy and the man, and when he came to work for me I've been away and left $20,000 in his hands without fear many a time. Gambler and sport and drunkard he was, but he never was accused of a crime, and through his life he was clean-handed. Then he took to the drink. I tried to stop him. He was working for me in Bleecker street then. The drink had a hold on him, and he couldn't stop. I had to discharge him, but we were always friends, and I was glad when Billy joined the Mission and reformed."

As he finished speaking his voice was uncertain and tears were in his eyes.

FROM GUTTER TO GLORY

Many strange and pathetic scenes have been witnessed in the old McAuley Mission down in Water Street, in the old Fourth Ward of New York City, but perhaps nothing could better illustrate the character of this work for saving poor lost souls than what took place some little time ago in that old haven. On stools in front of the platform rested a coffin, a very respectable one, too, with three massive silver handles on each side. A floral anchor lay in the centre, and at the foot was a sheaf of wheat. Inside the coffin lay the body of " Old Pop Lloyd." The face was peaceful and serene; there was no indication of the tempestuous life through which he had passed, but the look of calm repose spoke in eloquent tones, " Though I walk through the valley of the shadow of death, I will fear no evil; for Thou art with me; Thy rod and Thy staff they comfort me." On the platform was W. W. Bowdish, pastor of old John Street Methodist Church, "Old Pop's" pastor; also the Rev. Stephen Merritt, a dear friend of the Mission. The chapel was filled with mourners, converts of the Mission mostly. They were a grand set of men who had learned to love "Old Pop," and nearly everyone had come in the place just as he had, drunkards and homeless outcasts.

Many years ago "Pop Lloyd" came into the Mission one night and took a seat on the back bench. He was 72 years old, covered with rags and dirt and vermin, bent nearly double, and had not slept in a bed for weeks.

When the invitation was given to those who wished to seek the Saviour in the pardon of their sins, Mrs. Sarah Sherwood, the missionary, spoke to him and invited him forward. He asked her if she thought there was any hope for the worst man in New York. She said, "Yes; whosoever would might come." He came and was soundly converted to God. From that night he never touched whiskey or tobacco, which for years had been his chief articles of diet.

"Old Pop" had been a great character in his day. He was born on the high seas, and continued to rove them most all his early life, and once had the reputation of being a pretty successful buccaneer. He was once transported to Van Diemen's Land for ten years, and while in Australia was to be hung for murder, but made his escape. He had been quite well-to-do, and sailed his own vessel out of this port.

For the last three years of his life he could do nothing, and was a charge on the Mission; kind friends, with the aid of John Street Church, contributing to his support. He had drunk so much bad rum his vocal chords were burnt out and he could scarcely make himself understood, but he would often give his testimony in pantomime, stooping down low to show how the devil had him bent over when he came in the Mission, and then raising himself up erect to show how Christ took the load off a man's back and soul.

At seven o'clock in the morning he would come in the Mission and remain there all day. They would take him down three square meals each day, as his limbs were too weak to carry him upstairs. Many a time has the writer seen him give his meal to some poor tramp who had slipped in the door, much as a stray cat would do, looking for something to eat. No matter who they were, " Pop " would share his meal with them if they were hungry.

A few evenings before his death he arose with great difficulty and said, though he felt unworthy, he could say God was keeping him.

COLONEL ATKINSON

Here is Mr. Hadley's story of the Colonel:

" He was without doubt the most thorough-paced tramp that ever came into our old Mission, where the lost congregate in such numbers. No pen can adequately describe him, but we may be able to give a faint idea of how he looked. He was over six feet tall and sixty years old, but he looked a hundred. His beard was a dirty grey and a foot long. His hair, the same colour, hung down his back for a like length. His eyes were bleared and the hue of his face showed that water and he had long been strangers. He had on a ragged old overcoat, probably picked out of some ash barrel, and fastened with a nail; an old coat and vest completed his wardrobe. Of course, he had neither a shirt nor undershirt. His trousers were simply indescribable; they consisted of holes tied up with strings and a little cloth here and there. On his feet were pieces of carpet wrapped up with strings.

"I had known him for years as a common beggar. It was thirteen years ago last June when he came to see me one Sunday night, and he stood up for prayer in the middle of the service. Peering forward, he asked if I was present, and when I said, 'Yes,' he said, 'Mr. Hadley, pray for me. I am contrite.' At the invitation he came up with twenty others and prayed like a man in dead earnest. When we rose from our knees he stood up and said, 'Well, I am saved! There is no doubt about it.' At the close of the service he put his arm around my neck and said:

"'Brother Hadley, what ye going to give me?'

"'Oh,' said I, 'you will get a night's lodging.'

"'Yes,' said he, 'that's right; what else?'

"'I will give you a quarter for your breakfast,' said I.

"'That's right,' said he again, 'that's right. I always knowed you was a Christian,' and with his quarter and a ticket for bed, he tottered off.

"As he left me he said, 'I'll come every night.' 'Oh, don't,' I said, 'just come occasionally.' But he said again, 'Yes, Brother Hadley, I'll come every night.'

"Who was this man; this finished work of Satan's cruel power? He was from one of the best Ohio families; from a wealthy, prosperous Christian home. After college he studied law in the office of Edwin M. Stanton, the great War Secretary under Lincoln. He married and began to practise law, but in college he had learned to drink whiskey. He entered the army at the outbreak of the war, served through that fearful struggle with credit, and was mustered out a colonel of cavalry in an Illinois regiment, but a confirmed drunkard. He tried to struggle against that deadly habit which had securely fastened itself upon him, but it was useless. At last, when home was destroyed and wife and children gone, he became utterly discouraged. He came to New York, assumed another name, never went near the post office, and ultimately became a common beggar on the streets. For over a quarter of a century he had been a confirmed drunkard.

" This was the man who came up for prayers at the Water Street Mission. He was on hand early the next night, and when the invitation was given he came up with the rest, and after praying very unctuously rose up and said he was saved—sure, this time! He tried to put his arm around me again, but I repelled him with much more vigour than grace, I fear. I pointed him to the door.

" ' Do you mean it? ' said he.

" ' If you linger much longer,' said I, ' you'll see if I mean it.'

" He went slowly out cursing me and the Mission and everybody else, and swearing he would die in the street rather than come in again.

" I had been sorely tried that night. I had to put out three longshoremen, who came in drunk looking for a fight, and I was clearly a backslider. My heart smote me as I saw the miserable, hopeless figure go out into the night. I went to bed, but not to sleep. I could think of nothing else, pray for nothing else. I felt he must be saved or I would be lost.

"Two weeks from that day we had a monthly meeting of rescue workers. Our speaker had disappointed us, and someone said, 'Call on Brother Hadley.' I said, 'Yes, I have something to say to-day,' and with shame and weeping I told them about the old Colonel and how I had treated him. While I spoke it seemed as if the Holy Ghost fell on us all. No one said 'pray,' but all fell on their knees. They prayed for the Colonel and they prayed for me, that God would deliver my soul. While they prayed the light broke. 'Get up,' said I, 'you need not pray any more.' They gathered around me and said, 'Oh, Brother Hadley, have you got your answer?' 'I have,' said I, as I wrung their hands. I hastened to the elevated road and came down to the Mission, and there on the back bench sat the Colonel. It was my turn now, and I put my arms around his neck and burst into tears.

"I got him a beefsteak, bread, butter, potatoes and coffee, and he ate like a famished animal. I got a tub of hot water, a bar of soap and plenty of towels and clean clothes, and with the hands that pen these lines I washed this poor outcast. I dressed him from head to foot and took him over across the street to the barber's, and soon his long hair and beard disappeared. He stayed to the meeting and came forward; but how changed! His whole frame trembled with emotion and tears fell from his eyes to the floor as he cried, 'O Lord, if it ain't too late, forgive this lost sinner!'

" For six nights this was repeated, and on Saturday night he arose at the close of our service, and said with heaven in his face, ' Oh, Brother Hadley, I am saved.' I said, ' I believe you,' and then we did have a hug.

" From that instant the old beggar tramp was turned into a child of God. He fairly loathed rum and all its works. God restored to him his intellect, which was so sadly impaired; his youth returned, and he became a tall, dignified, handsome Christian gentleman.

" Thousands have heard him, during the last thirteen years, tell in the most convincing manner how Jesus had reached down and saved him and kept him. For some time past his health had been failing, and at last we put him in the Presbyterian Hospital. On February 28 he went to see Jesus, whom he loved so well. He was buried from our dear old Water Street Mission.

" ' For I will be merciful to their unrighteousness, and their sins and their iniquities will I remember no more.' HEBREWS viii. 12."

I knew the Colonel intimately. " I think I never saw a nobler specimen of manhood. " Tell us," I said to him one evening, " about your old life and your new experience." Straightening himself up, he said, " Two words will describe them both. The old life was *hell*; the new life is *heaven*."

The funeral services of Harry McQuillan, one of the Cranest of the Crane in the army of old England, Harry McQuillan, who won the Victoria Cross, were held in December, 1904, at the dear old Mission.

He enlisted when a young man in the Seventy-seventh Prince of Wales Regiment, belonging to the Second Brigade, Light Division, under command of General Sir George Brown, in the Crimean War; took part in the battles of the Alma, the capture of Balaklava, and the battle of Inkermann, the siege and storm of Sebastopol. He was brought under special notice of the Commander in Chief, Lord Raglan, for bravery on the field, and on returning to England was brought to the notice of Her Majesty, Queen Victoria, at Aldershot. He was sent to Australia and from there to India to suppress the Mutiny, where, in 1857, Brother McQuillan was present at Cawnpur, Lucknow, at the capture of Lucknow, and also at the siege of Delhi. He stood guard at the famous well of Cawnpur, where some 375 women and children were thrown after their butchery by the savages.

For years he had been known as "Old Harry" on the Bowery, sleeping in hallways, trucks, parks, for months, and on a supper night came into the mission and heard that Jesus could save a drunkard, and he gave his heart to the only one who could save him, and for many years led a good Christian life, and died in the Methodist Hospital, Brooklyn. There was no volley for the hero, over his grave, but his comrades in the new life stood around the grave, lifting up their voices in song and praise and prayer, for he had won even a greater victory in his latter years than he did on the battlefield; conquered through the grace and strength of Jesus, the appetite and passion of the life of sin.

XII

AT NORTHFIELD AND WINONA

S. H. HADLEY was devoted to D. L. Moody, and he had the entire confidence of this distinguished evangelist, who rarely made a mistake in his estimate of men, and who never lost an opportunity to say a good word concerning the greatest rescue mission worker of his generation. He has been present at almost every Northfield Conference for the past ten or twelve years. Great Bible teachers might interest the Northfield audience; S. H. Hadley always thrilled them. He was usually given the Round Top meeting, and it was here that he was always at his best. Stories of remarkable conversion he was always ready to tell, but he uniformly closed with his own testimony, and never lost an opportunity to tell how Jesus had saved him and through the many years had graciously kept him.

After D. L. Moody's death, his interest seemed to deepen in the work which was carried on by Mr. William R. Moody, and he repeatedly said: "I must do all I can for Will; he has a heavy load to carry, and if by going to Northfield I can lighten it in the least, I feel called upon to go."

He usually came from Northfield to Winona, and from the very first Conference to the one held a year ago, in 1905, he was an honoured speaker. Great theologians, wonderful expositors of the Word of

God, successful evangelists and preachers of renown might be announced, but whenever it was known that S. H. Hadley was to speak the people with one accord rushed to hear him. The hymn he loved to sing at Winona was "Oh, It Is Wonderful," and it was unique to see the staid, conservative Christians singing this song over and over under his strange leadership. One evening when F. B. Meyer was present as speaker, Mr. Hadley led the congregational singing by beating time with his cane, and the people sang until the building seemed to echo and re-echo with the music.

One day at Winona he was in attendance upon a ministerial conference. The ministers were trying to decide what was essential on the part of a minister in order that he should be well qualified to preach. It was finally decided that a knowledge of Greek was exceedingly helpful. Mr. Hadley paid the closest of attention, and just as the meeting was about to adjourn, he rose slowly and said: "See here, where do I come in? I do not know one Greek letter from another, and yet I can preach as good a sermon as any of you, and a good deal better than some of you. This discussion makes me sick," he said with a smile. "It is not essential that you should know Greek, but you should know the Lord. Why, brethren," said he, "I heard of an old man in the South who preached a sermon from the text of Scripture, 'He that is not with me, is against me; and he that gathereth not with me, scattereth abroad,' and because he could not read he quoted it incorrectly, 'He that is not with me, is against me, and he that gathereth not with me, scratcheth a board.'" He said the old preacher went on describing how if any man should reject Jesus Christ he would have to scratch a board all through eternity; told how he would get slivers in his fingers until they were sore and festered, and yet he would have to go on scratching. When it was over the mourners' bench was filled with seekers. "More," he said, "I doubt not than many of you preachers ever have had through all of your ministry." Shouting with laughter, every minister present decided that S. H. Hadley had gotten the best of them, and that after all the secret of preaching was to know Christ.

We have always observed his birthday at .Winona, August 27. Assisted by his special friends in rescue mission work—Harry Monroe, Melvin Trotter, John Callahan and W. M. Bruce—from time to time during the Conference he conducted great rescue mission services. The crowds attending these services were the largest of any during the entire Conference. But when the 27th day of August came, his rescue mission friends, the ministers present, all the people on the grounds and the near-by city of Warsaw, delighted to do him honour.

Every year he would tell the story of his conversion, and just when the time seemed opportune during his testimony it was my privilege to say that I believed the time had come when we should make him a birthday offering, for Water Street Mission, and at the suggestion money would literally be showered upon him. Hundreds of people would pass by attempting to shake his hand, but he was wise enough to know that he would have more than his pockets full of money, so he would hold his hat with both hands and sing as the people passed, "Oh, It Is Wonderful."

The service went on increasing in enthusiasm until the hat was full of money, and it was always a question as to who was the happier, S. H. Hadley or the people who gave to him on this occasion. Said a distinguished preacher at the close of one of these birthday meetings, " I now understand what it means to be a ' hilarious giver.' "

The Conference of 1906 will be held without him. He is in the presence of the King, but so long as the present management is in control the 27th day of August will be observed as S. H. Hadley's birthday service and someone from Water Street will be present to tell of him, " Who being dead, yet speaketh."

Every summer for the past seven years at the Winona Bible Conference six distinguished rescue missionaries have met together to confer about their work, to pray for the outcast, and to give their faithful testimonies not only concerning their own conversion, but the salvation of hundreds and thousands of others lost and ruined like themselves, who have found the Saviour.

These missionaries were:

S. H. Hadley, New York City.

Harry Monroe, Chicago, Ill.

Melvin Trotter, Grand Rapids, Mich.

W. M. Bruce, Louisville, Ky.

J. P. Callahan, New York City.

W. V. Wheeler, Indianapolis, Ind.

I have written to these missionaries asking them to write me a line concerning S. H. Hadley, and they have responded as follows:

" One of the greatest blessings that ever came into my life was my first meeting with Brother Hadley a

S. H. HADLEY SPEAKING AT WINONA.

number of years ago, at a Christian Worker's Convention in Chicago. The gathering was not large, so those in attendance had a splendid opportunity of personal acquaintance and fellowship.

"As the days were given to rehearsal of Christian work, and discussion of ways and means of doing the same, one could easily get a glimpse into the inner life of those engaged in the rescue of the lost. At the head of all those most interested and whose soul was aflame with love for his fellowmen, stood dear Brother Hadley. As he spoke to the audience, his face bathed in tears, his voice tender and sweet, he touched them with a love divine and created within them a great desire to possess the same passion for souls which was so mightily his.

" One had to stand shoulder to shoulder with him in his pleadings with the lost to appreciate how real Christ was to Him and how completely he lived upon the Word of God. It was my great privilege to see him, as by appointment from this convention three of us held a service in the country jail! He began by inviting the men to come to him when released. He said: 'Now, I'll give you a password; when you come use it: if you are hungry, I'll feed you; if you need clothes, I'll provide you these, and if you need a friend, come to me.' At the invitation a great many thronged to the altar to accept Christ.

" He lived and practised his favourite text, ' And the servant of the Lord must not strive; but be gentle unto all men, apt to teach, patient in meekness, instructing those that oppose themselves; if God peradventure will give them repentance to acknowledging of the truth, and that they may recover themselves out of the snare of the devil, who are taken captive by him at his will.' 11 Tim. ii. 24-26. Also, ' But love ye your enemies and do good, and lend, hoping for nothing again, and your reward shall be great, and ye shall be the children of the Highest; for He is kind unto the unthankful and to the evil.' St. Luke vi. 35.

"Love and kindness stood out in bold relief, affecting alike the Christian, whose peace was made with God, and the weary sin-sick man who had come to believe no one cared for his soul until he heard and met this true embassador of the most High. How I thank God for meeting and working with this man of God, whose wonderful life has been and is a constant inspiration to me, not only to love God with a truer devotion and do His will more perfectly, but to seek more diligently the lost. Thank God for my fellowship with Him.

" JOHN CALLAHAN."

" CHICAGO, April 25, 1906.

"I am very happy to give my impressions of our beloved Brother Hadley. The 13th chapter of First Corinthians has always been a gem of rare beauty to me. I have read commentaries upon it, but never fully understood its interpretation until I met S. H. Hadley at a convention of Christian workers at Tremont Temple, in Boston, November, 1892. And while others may wonder at the secret of his marvellous success, I discovered on that occasion that he possessed a passion born of God for souls that equipped him for what has proved a most remarkable ministry.

"Like his Master, he loved everybody, and more particularly he seemed to be in heaven when on his knees with some poor crushed sinner telling the precious story of how Jesus came into the world to heal the broken-hearted and bind up their wounds. Hadley was what might be called in the business world a plunger. He believed that none had fallen so low but that the 'precious blood of Jesus' could cleanse and purify their lives. When others might be disposed to pass upon some poor broken-down bum or thief, Hadley believed there was nothing too hard for the Lord and would lift and lift and lift, and follow the wayward with prayer and acts of kindness to the end, and then stand by the open grave like Jesus did of old and weep because he could do no more.

"Brother Hadley was one of the most transparent men I have ever known. Every moment of his life he was conscious of the presence of Jesus, in whom he lived and moved and had his being. While an enthusiast, he believed in bringing things to pass. He was wonderfully sane and never was diverted by men or issues from the sweet simple story of how Jesus saved him, a poor dying sinner.

"As a rescue mission worker he was a genius, and his power of manipulating the lives of men who live in what is known as the slum district of our cities was a marvel. 'The love of God' shed abroad in his heart gave him a magnetism that always made him attractive whether in the slums of New York praying with a broken-down bum, or in some swell uptown church telling the people on easy street how the good Lord saved him.

"He was always natural. While perhaps few men in his day have been more highly honoured in association with great men, yet you would always find him

the same humble, unassuming, loving Hadley, prefer-
ring always to work in the shadow than in the lime-
light, where others love to shine. He was in a class
by himself.

"Endowed by nature with a striking personality,
genial and optimistic, a man who had the faculty of
making friends on sight, when our brother got a
vision of ' the Christ,' and ' old things passed away and
all things became new,' Jesus made S. H. Hadley a
bearer of good news and hope to thousands of lost and
hopeless men and women, who have been ' saved by
grace and kept by the power of God.'

"Personally his life and labours have been a great
inspiration to me. Since he has been called home I
have felt as though I lost a brother indeed. He was
a true friend. This all Christian workers will concede,
and more particularly rescue mission workers. He
believed in giving every body a square deal.

"Sincerely yours,

"HARRY MONROE."

"GRAND RAPIDS, MICH., April 16, 1906.

"I first met S. H. Hadley at Northfield, Mass., six
years ago. I heard him speak at Round Top; got
down in front of him where I could see his face and
the first look that I got of him my heart went out to
him and I loved him ever since. As he told the story
of his life, I cried like a child. I had suffered from
the same sin. At once I began to search for his power.
I talked with him about his work and about mission
work generally, but did not tell him I was a mission
man. I wanted to learn his methods and the secret of
his power. In Chicago the next winter, where we

were together at a Christian Worker's Convention, I saw a practical demonstration of it. I found his power lay in his love for souls and his love of souls came from his love of Christ and the vision that comes by the baptism of the Holy Ghost; so I reasoned it this way: to love the unlovely as S. H. Hadley does one must have the love of God shed abroad in his heart by the Holy Ghost. I saw him talking to a man that was drunk and slipped up close to him and listened to what he said, and he stood there and wept over that stranger that was drunk.

" I turned from him and went alone before God and stayed there until God gave me the same power. I used to try to love souls and I did win some for Jesus, but after S. H. Hadley came into my life I did not have to try, God put the love there.

" The first time he heard me give my testimony he came to me after the service and put his arm about my neck and told me that while I didn't know very much I knew enough to love Jesus and love souls, and then he gave me advice that I have lived and followed, and if I have been a success as a mission worker it was largely due to this first heart to heart talk with S. H. Hadley. I came home from the convention and changed my methods of working. I carried a great deal of gunpowder in my make-up, and I could fight sometimes easier than I could pray, but the love of God and love for souls has enabled me to see Christ-likeness, or at least a soul for whom Christ died, in the very lowest drunkard in the gutter. I thank God for Hadley's life; I thank God for the victory in his death, and I think if there is one man who will live on and on, it is dear old ' Hopp ' Hadley.

"Each summer for ten days at Winona I have followed him around from place to place, catching from him some of the sweetest glimpses of my Lord that I have ever had. He was very kind to me, making me presents of books that he thought would help me, and writing me off and on for the last six years letters of encouragement. He wasn't afraid to pay a little compliment here and there, and every move he would make seemed to endear him more and more in my life.

"He was to be with me at my anniversary, January 19, 20 and 21 of this year, and on the morning of the 18th, because of his illness, he wired me that it would be impossible for him to come. The telegram was a long one and the letter that followed explaining his trouble and sickness was, I think, the sweetest letter I have ever received from any man. It was so full of love and so full of Christ that it just seemed, as I read it to my people, that there wasn't a dry eye in the house.

"If Hadley could say nothing good of anyone, he wouldn't say anything. When I heard of a criticism coming from one of the ministers in Winona about Hadley and his gang of 'bums' speaking from the platform, all he said was, 'The Lord help him. He ought to come down to Water Street and let the Lord save him.' Turning to me he said, 'You old bum. You love Jesus and love souls and that combination makes a devil-possessed preacher turn green with envy. Some of 'em are too dead to skin.'

"After telling the story one day at Winona, he said to me, after having spoken to three or four thousand people in the auditorium, 'Trotter, it's too bad they ain't all "bums," so we could lead them to Jesus.'

S. H. HADLEY AND CHARLES M. ALEXANDER AT
NORTHFIELD.

Little did he know what his words of encouragement meant to me.

" I was a drunkard when Jesus saved me, and many people seemed to see very much good in me, but Hadley made me feel that I amounted to something in the Kingdom of God. He used to say, ' We mission bums are a part of God's aristocracy.' When I have been tempted to feel that my work for Him amounted to nothing I would always go back to the time that Sam Hadley told me I was a ' winner ' because I loved the drunkard.

" I am a better man for having loved S. H. Hadley, and my prayer is that God may raise up someone to take the place of this man in this old, wicked world. The drunkards of this country have lost their best friend in the death of S. H. Hadley. He has put rescue mission work where it is in this country to-day. May the Lord bless his memory.

" MELVIN E. TROTTER."

" LOUISVILLE, KY., July 3, 1906.

" I am very glad to pay a loving tribute to the memory of the friend of sinners, Samuel Hopkins Hadley. His noble and lovable character and life endeared him to the cultured and wealthy, as well as to the depraved and poor. To us, however, whom he led up from the depths to know the grace and love of God, his life was a true benediction and his death causes keenest sorrow; yet we rejoice because we know he is now with Jesus, whom he so truly loved and served.

" The first time I met S. H. Hadley was at the second anniversary of his appointment as superintendent of the McAuley Water Street Mission, which I attended as a spectator with a party of friends from the church to which I belonged. At that time I was a prosperous lawyer, and although not a Christian, was a teacher in one of the large Sunday Schools in New York City.

"Five years or six years later, when I was a poor, helpless, sinful drunkard, having lost money, business, self-respect, and everything worth having in this life, except the love of a sainted mother and noble wife, who would not let me go, vile though I was, I met dear Brother Hadley again. From that time began a close and tender relationship that grew more and more precious every year. I was hopeless, penniless and miserable. Instead of upbraiding, he helped me; he told me of Jesus's love and power to save. I resolved to quit drink and lead a better life. For a while I did fairly well, but because I would not make a full surrender, soon fell lower than before. When in trouble, like thousands of others, I thought of Hadley, who was so well known as the friend of the man in trouble. I went to him and he again pointed me to Jesus. I tried his patience more perhaps than anyone else, being an obstinate man, unwilling to yield my will to God. Dear Brother Hadley never lost patience with any sinner and never gave a man up. Thank God, he held on to me. I remember one occasion when I went to him in an awful plight. At first he did not recognise me; then he looked at me with disgust for my sinful condition; then lifting his eyes to mine with an expression of sadness, tenderness and sympathy on his dear face, he said, ' Bruce, give it all up to God.' I am so glad I did so and for many years have been striving to give it all up to God. I have not had a closer earthly friend than S. H. Hadley. For over ten years he has been my confidant, with whom I could freely advise about the difficulties and trials as well as the joys and successes of the work the Master has given me. His influence upon my life has been deeper and stronger than that of any other man. Whatever success as a soul-winner I have had, is due in a very large measure to the Christlike example of S. H. Hadley.

"The last time I saw him was at Winona, in August, 1905, when we had our last quiet talk together. He spoke of heaven and said: 'It won't be long until you and I are there.' He has gone to the better country. What a multitude of redeemed drunkards, saved through his instrumentality, welcomed him as he reached the Golden Shore. Multitudes are following after who will greet him there when to them this life is over. I am looking forward to that time when the Master shall say to me, 'It is enough, come home.'

"Yours sincerely,

"WM. M. BRUCE."

XIII

SPECIAL MESSAGES

ONE day in moving some articles in my home I came across a phonograph and packed in with it a number of old records. Calling my children about me I put on one of these records and started the phonograph going, when, to my perfect surprise, I heard the voice of one of the members of my household who for three years had been in heaven. Five years before the record of the voice had been made and for the first time in three years we heard the voice of the loved one who was gone. The effect was startling and one could scarcely say pleasing.

S. H. Hadley being dead yet speaketh, but his words have quite the opposite effect upon us from the message in the phonograph. In these messages of his we see his great heart and we understand something of the mighty principles which governed him in his life work. We also catch a glimpse of the depth of his passion for souls and there is given to us the clearest possible picture of his devotion to the poor, lost outcasts of society.

OUR WORK

Our work is entirely with the lost who have squandered all long ago, and are for the most part dying on the streets or in the low groggeries of the neighbourhood. They are in a condition when they come here **that** would be impossible to describe. No language can portray it. It must be seen to be believed. Such men must have care of all kinds, clothing, food, medicine and lodging; are often sent to the hospital for a long or short period; in fact, it is real, genuine mission work, and plenty of it, and it all takes money to care for it. If anyone would doubt this, let him come down and take a look at the converts any night, and their testimonies will leave no doubt about the condition they were in when they came here, and how they are now, since Christ has done His work in their hearts.

In some Christian movements they try to save nice sinners, well-dressed sinners and sinners with good moral characters, but with us it is quite the contrary. We think the worst need salvation the most and so we seek the very worst. Thank God, they cannot be too bad for Him. Our testimonies are all clear, convincing and spiritual. They deal with present salvation. One brother says, "Now, you may think the last drink I took was a good one, when I only gave five cents for it, and it has lasted me sixteen years. Praise the Lord, I haven't wanted to take a drink or ' chaw of tobacky' since I knelt down then and asked God to save my soul; I got up a saved man. How do I know I was saved? Why, if you had a heavy load on your back would you not know when it dropped off? They used to call me ' Old Bill,' but now it is Mr. Love."

TESTIMONIES

The main feature of our service is now as always the testimonies of the converts. Night after night, year in and year out, this sweetest music sounds in our ears. It never grows tiresome. How strange! These testimonies are very practical and deal in one way or another with all the affairs of life. One brother said: "I had no money, I had no clothes. How can a man have money when he has no clothes? But how is it to-day? I ain't a dead man to-day, I am worth a dozen dead men. I have clothes, have furniture, and money, too. I don't want any whiskey now. I have Jesus, and He satisfies my longing as nothing else can do." All these men testify in a plain, common-sense way. Their story is stripped almost entirely of all cant phrases. "I came into this Mission," say they, "so long ago (giving the exact number of years, months and days). I was a drunkard and had been for years. I was in rags, half dead, so tired I knew not what to do. I had 'carried the banner' (walked streets all night) for months. I heard some-one speak about this place in a gin mill where I was hanging out, so I came down. I heard the boys here tell about Jesus, how He loved them and how He had saved them. They said Jesus was the sinner's friend. They had been drunkards just like me. In fact, I had known some of the men I saw here in some of the institutions where I had been. Well, I made up my mind I would make a start; I hadn't any feeling at all, but I wanted help and wanted it bad, so I came forward and knelt down and asked Jesus to save my poor, lost soul. I tell you He has done it. I don't drink any whiskey now. Praise the Lord! I don't want it. That old appetite has been taken away. I don't know where to find it. I reckon I could find it if I would go hanging around the saloons, but I have had enough of that old life. I have work now and every comfort I need, and it is Jesus who has done it all." There, brother, sister, this is typical Water Street testimony.

In 1901, in the *Homiletic Review*, there appeared an article, " Some Principles of Rescue Work," in which the author strongly objected to the testimony of redeemed drunkards. Mr. Hadley felt at once called upon to answer this article, and he wrote as follows:

" Testimony is not a new thing, by any means. King David testified far more plainly than I have ever heard anyone do in any meeting that I have ever attended. He gave utterance to such soul-stirring psalms as ' Bless the Lord, Oh My Soul,' but he also, in the bitterness of his soul, left on the imperishable pages of Holy Writ such expressions as: ' My wounds stink and are corrupt because of my foolishness.' Psalm xxxviii. 5.

" In the fifth chapter of Mark we read of the poor woman who had an issue of blood for twelve years and could find no help. She stole behind Jesus and clutched the hem of his garment, and was made whole instantly. She was going to keep quiet about it, but the dear Master would not have it so. Under the Jewish law this woman was unclean, and should not have come into contact with anyone; but Jesus called her, and she came trembling and fell before Him, and told Him before all that crowd of people, men and women, on the public street, ' all the truth.' Jesus sealed this honest confession by a blessing on her head and calling her 'daughter.' In the same chapter hear what Jesus said to the demoniac, out of whom the legions of devils had been cast. When he wanted to follow his precious new found Friend, Jesus said, ' Go home to thy friends and tell them how great things the Lord hath done for thee, and how He had mercy upon thee.'

" I have been living in rescue missions almost ever since my conversion, over nineteen years ago, and have heard tens of thousands of testimonies; I have never heard one that would shock the decent ears of any Christian woman who was a friend to sinners. I have been in the Florence Crittenton Mission over a thousand times, where the testimonies are chiefly by redeemed women. I have heard them tell, with streaming eyes, how Jesus had saved them from a life of shame and sorrow, and with nothing suggestive of anything unwholesome or unbecoming. One of the grandest workers I know of among the lost is a person who had been a thorough-paced man of the world and had sunken down in sin, and was saved in the Florence Mission, one night nearly seventeen years ago, while I was there, by hearing just such a testimony as I have described. This is by no means an isolated case. I have attended testimony meetings at Mrs. Whittemore's Door of Hope time and again, and at the Wayside Home, in Brooklyn, and have heard the sweet story of rescue and salvation from the lips of the redeemed ones, and never a word to offend.

" I was saved by the testimony of redeemed men, and it is a sensitive subject with me. On April 23, 1882, I went into Jerry McAuley's Mission, a dying drunkard. I had just come from the station house, where I had gone to have myself locked up with delirium tremens. I had never been in a rescue mission before; and there I saw Jerry McAuley stand up before a crowd of ladies and gentlemen and sinners of every type, and he said, ' I am saved to-night from whiskey and tobacco and everything that's wicked and bad. I used to be a regular old bum and a thief down in the Fourth Ward, but Jesus came into me and took the whole thing out of me, and I don't want it any more.' Never had I heard anything like this. I had heard people tell how good they were, but the candour of this man convinced me it was real. Then Sister McAuley stood up and said she had been saved from a life of drunkenness and shame by the precious Saviour fourteen years before and had been kept sweetly ever since, and the great tears of love rolled down her cheeks. I said, 'I wonder if I can't be saved?' and I was saved that night and have been kept saved ever since."

"OUR GUESTS

" Not infrequently it is true that special attention is paid the rich in places of public worship; the man with the goodly apparel and the gold ring is many times shown the preference in the matter of attention and the assigning of a seat, but this is not true at Water Street.

" One night a leading lawyer with his cultured wife came to the Mission. They came out of curiosity, but in the service they were convicted of sin. They both belonged to the very best class of society in New York, but when they raised their hands for prayers and acknowledged themselves to be sinners they were told that they must bow with the rest at the altar, and from their knees they entered into an experience of power to which up to that time they had been strangers.

" The thing that has impressed us most during the past year above all else is the wonderful love of Jesus for poor, helpless, dying men. Hundreds who came in here were so nearly dead—they seemed almost incapable of exercising a bit of faith, or comprehending what was said—but when we would get down on our knees before God, somehow the day began to break, and they would feel their load of sin and cry to Jesus for help.

" It is impossible to carry on this work without assisting those who come, more or less. A man can exist somehow, hanging around a saloon, no matter how ragged or dirty he is, but when he tries to get up he is powerless to do so, unless some friendly hand is extended to give him the aid he so much needs. We are here to save the worst, the vilest, and the most degraded on earth, and we love to see that kind come in preference to all others.

" GOD IS WITH US

" We have men who came to us drunkards and were converted, many women who came here drunkards and were converted to God, and they have made for themselves good homes, gone into business, prospered, and employ others and contribute to our work; hundreds of dollars are paid every year for the support of this work by men and women who could not have raised one penny when they came here unless they had stolen or begged it. While many of our converts go away to home or friends, and find employment that takes them out of our reach, we always have a good crowd at the Mission service. We hardly ever have less than twenty-five redeemed men present, and often fifty. Our congregation will average over seventy-five men the year round; and as many of our converts become earnest workers we have lively meetings. Then we do have to a remarkable and precious degree the power of the Holy Ghost at all our services. Don't take our word for it, but come and see. 'The best of all, God is with us.' We have learned long since that without Him we can do nothing. We have never lowered the standard one inch. We believe and proclaim that Jesus, and Jesus only, can save a sinner from eternal perdition, and believing this mighty truth, we work in season and out of season to persuade men to turn away from lives of sin and sorrow and come to our blessed Saviour and find eternal life. We think it a great privilege to be able and have a chance to do this. 'Do your men fall?' How often I have been asked that question. Yes, I am sorry to say they do fall, many of them and often fall many times, but we never give a man up. We have never yet had a chance to test the full measure of Jesus' loving commandment to forgive seventy times seven. It would be a wonder if they did not fall. Almost insane and ready to drop from excess, want and exposure, ready to die on their feet for want of sleep and care, every drop of blood in their bodies calling for alcohol, which has been their steady diet for years; every friend or acquaintance they know is a drunkard. Saloon doors on every hand wide open, warm, brilliantly lighted and inviting. Is it any wonder they fall? We think it a matter to rejoice over if they don't fall. When our men fall all the world knows it, but not so with a well-contained and sober sinner.

"WHAT THE MISSION IS

" Many come to us for the sole purpose of obtaining employment; but this we discourage, for we believe most men who come here are idle because they are drunkards and not trustworthy. We believe that the Lord has a job for every saved drunkard, as soon as He sees it is safe for him to have it. We believe the blessed old book, the Bible, and every promise in it.

"One of our sheet anchors is, ' Seek ye first the Kingdom of God and His righteousness, and all these things shall be added.' MATT. vi. 33.

"In answer to many inquiries, verbally and by letter, we wish to say that the McAuley Mission is not a university settlement, a labour bureau, or any of the new-fangled plans to simply better the condition of the human race; but it is a real, low-down rescue work, and consequently is the highest work in the city. The most degraded men and women in the world are the most welcome to our doors, which stand open night and day. If they are homeless we will be a home to them; if friendless, we will be their friend; if hungry (as they all are), we feed them; if naked, we clothe them; if without character, we will lead them to One who makes character. We have nothing to offer here here but Jesus the crucified one. We believe that one look at that bleeding victim would transform the vilest sinner and make him white as snow. Of this class are made up the great army men and women who were saved in McAuley Mission. We believe in the old-time religion—the dear old gospel—salvation through the blood has never failed and it never will fail. Hallelujah!

"AN ILLUSTRATION

"One peculiar character who came to Water Street was Henry Miller, alias Slippery Dick. He was a German, a small man, smooth, clean and tidy; did not take much to liquor, but a born thief. I met him years ago, in 1884, in Mike Dunn's home for ex-convicts. I got to like him very much. He went to prison several times after this and has served altogether thirty-six years behind the bars. He began coming in here several years ago, and used all his arts on the writer to beat him out of all he could; and I must say with a great deal of success. I found that no ordinary methods would do for Slippery Dick, so I gave him about everything he asked for, and he went off with a chuckle, satisfied that he had at last found a sucker; but don't you know, dear reader, that the devil often gets beaten at his own game, and Slippery Dick finally got so ashamed at the way he treated me and the way I treated him, that he finally came up for prayers to our mercy seat and said, when he rose from his knees, ' I have been trying to be a Christian for a good many years, but I am going to quit trying now; I am going to be a Christian and I am not going to take anything from Mr. Hadley if I starve in the street.' He went out that night and carried the banner (walked the streets) ; the next day he went to the Rev. Mr. Hudson, who has charge of some restaurants on the Bowery, and said, ' I want work, and if you don't give me work I will rob you.' Mr. Hudson looked at him, sized him up well, and said, ' Who are you?' He said, ' I am Slippery Dick, one of the biggest thieves in this town, but I made a resolution at the Old McAuley Mission to live a Christian life, and I am a thief no longer, but I must have work.'

" Mr. Hudson put him to washing dishes for two and a half dollars a week, and his room and board. He had a man as cashier who came to him with a string

of recommendations, and who had always been good
and honest, according to his tale, but this man robbed
him of every cent he could lay his hands on, and ran
away; then Mr. Hudson concluded that as the honest
man had robbed him so completely, he would see what
the thief would do; so he put in Slippery Dick as
cashier. He was true and honest to his trust. Slippery Dick got a bad cold, and I got him in the Presbyterian Hospital, and while everything was done that
could be done, our dear brother went home, and as he
was not afraid to die, he passed away in peace, fully
trusting in Jesus.

"LOVE FOR THE DRUNKARD

"How the writer, who is himself a redeemed drunkard, saved in Jerry's Mission by Christ alone at death's
door, does sympathise with the drunkard! Won't you
too, dear reader? Poor, helpless fellow, he does look
hard and dirty, don't he? No friends, no clothes, no
money; not a friend in the world. How glad I am to
be his friend and point him to the Lamb of God that
taketh away the sins of the world.

"'That head hath been pillowed on tenderest breast,
  That form hath been wept o'er, those lips have been pressed;
  That soul hath been prayed for in tones sweet and mild,
  For her sake deal gently with some mother's child.'

He was once bright, strong, willing and able to do his
part, but the saloon got his heart and life; he has
tried ever so hard, only to fail, but we love him and
Jesus can help him.

"'Poisoned by alcohol, blear-eyed and illy clad,
  Cursing his fate as he shuffled along;
  Crushed, and bereft of the once earnest will he had,
  Penniless, homeless, jeered by the throng.
  Friends have assisted him, pastors have prayed o'er him
  He has been rescued and lost o'er and o'er;
  Oh, do not give him up,
  Pull from his lips the cup,
  Speak to him kindly and try him once more.'

"HOW WE DO IT

"We do not preach or meddle; we do not denounce, arraign or persecute; we do not insist that others shall think as we do, or be as we are, or practise our precepts. This Mission offers a refuge for the fallen and abandoned. It helps those to rise who cannot rise in their own strength. It applies to the suffering and destitute the touch of sympathy and loving kindness. To the broken heart we offer hope. To the wasted life we offer encouragement and opportunity. To moral death we offer resurrection through Jesus Christ alone.

"We proclaim no dogmas, establish no theology, inflict no penalties. The Old Jerry McAuley Mission has no creeds or rituals. We are devoted to love and tender ministration; to help, and hope and rescue. Our missionaries see the misery and degradation at our own doors, and we hear the cry of the afflicted within our reach, and help all who come to our sacred altar.

"We recognise the claim of the neighbour's anguish upon our conscience and we arise and endeavour to help them. We believe our mission was sanctioned from the Mount of Olives, and we have pledged our lives and strength and love, everything within us, to lift up the fallen, cheer the faint, feed the hungry and clothe the naked.

"Is it discouraging? you ask. Oh, yes, it is simply heart-breaking from a human point of view, but all of us who work here have been saved ourselves out of the horrible pit, with the very smell of fire on our garments. We, too, have stooped down and drank out of the bitter stream, and we can sympathise with those who come to us with conscience seared and hearts broken, almost destitute, reputation and character gone, but we believe the loving touch of Jesus will restore life and manhood and womanhood. 'I am the resurrection and the life,' said He; 'he that believeth on Me, though he were dead yet shall he live; and whosoever liveth and believeth in Me shall never die," and we have seen this exemplified almost daily during the last eighteen years.

"Few people come here directly for salvation. Their needs drive them here. They have spent all and began to be in want. Thousands of them say, 'I will arise and go to my Father and say, Father, I have sinned against heaven and in Thy sight, and am no more worthy to be called Thy son,' and God the Father sees them a great way off.

"No one can deny that this work is trying. It drives us to the very last ditch. We cannot discriminate much; in fact we don't try. We help everybody who comes to us, more or less; in fact, we don't know who to refuse, for those who from the human standpoint seem the most hopeless turn out to be the brightest cases. Do they fall? Yes, alas, they do, and they rise again, and it's the same old story. Weak humanity, yielding to the mighty power of sin, and then Jesus comes in and helps them. Often we find men are better for this schooling in the end.

"The devil is the best missionary we get around Water Street. When a man gets on his feet, gets a good job, gets to feel that he don't need the Mission so much, he wanders around evenings, goes on the Bowery, goes into the play-house; then it is an easy step to the saloon. Then he goes down and Satan stamps on him with both feet, and within twenty-four hours his clothes are gone. His money gone too, and then he comes back to Water Street, half dead, and although it is discouraging, he has perhaps learned a lesson. Humbly and sincerely he starts again in the Christian life."

XIV

'AS 'AN EDITOR[1]

I N 1883, when Mr. Hadley first became associated with Jerry McAuley, it was decided to establish a newspaper. This paper was intended, not only to keep the interests of the McAuley Mission before the public, but it was given such circulation as to enable Jerry McAuley and his faithful co-worker to reach as many of the outcasts as possible,—those who would not read the ordinary newspaper; those who were behind prison bars who would be interested in the publication simply because it was published by one who had himself been in prison, and edited by one who was redeemed from the curse of strong drink.

WHY THE NAME WAS CHOSEN

" The editor of this paper was converted at Jerry McAuley's Mission. If he had not in God's mercy found his way to this place, he would not have been alive to start the *Perpetual Revival*. The object of this paper is to tell to the world the wonderful news of how God is blessing mission work in this city at this and other places. There are thousands of men

---

[1] I am indebted to Mr. Smith Allen of New York City for the old file of the *Perpetual Revival*. Mr. Allen was one of Mr. Hadley's devoted friends, a man who has stood by him in his work from the very first.　　　　J. W. C.

who have never heard the ' glad tidings,' and would be glad to attend these places where the nightly testimonies are so convincing, where high and low, rich and poor meet on a common level, where demonination and creed are forgotten. These are places where a burglar need not be ashamed to tell of his past life and ask for prayers and assistance. The drunkard who wants to reform can come in and be welcome whether he has a coat to his back or not. If he has none, they will pray for him and give him one.

" It was an untrodden field in journalism, and the result of three weeks' experience is that the *Perpetual Revival* has sprung into unheard of popularity, and it is not confined to those who make a profession alone. ' The boys ' like to read it. People who never go to church subscribe for it, saints and sinners take it, and when they have read it, send it to their friends in other cities and states, until now we are receiving letters from all parts of the United States asking for the *Revival*. In its columns will always be found a correct report of the doings and happenings at Jerry McAuley's Mission and other missions, as the interest of the work seems to warrant.

" Many have asked, ' Where did you get the name for your paper? ' The name is suggested from the fact that there has been a perpetual revival in progress at the Cremorne Mission ever since the writer was converted there, shortly after the Mission opened its doors nearly one year ago. The revival sprung up itself. It was the Holy Spirit moving on men's hearts, and as time goes on it increases. It will be the pleasant duty of this paper to chronicle these incidents in a newsy way which will be interesting to everyone."

In the various editorials there is given another view into the deep heart experience of S. H. Hadley. His views of mission work in general, his appreciation of the rescue mission, his abhorrence of strong drink, and his devotion to his Master, are all clearly portrayed in the editorials he prepared February 10.

" BAXTER STREET

" One thing that astonishes the young Christian more than anything else is to find so many good men and women where he did not expect to find any. Also, to see how much good is being done where he supposes the name of Christ was never spoken, except in blasphemy.

" As the writer was meandering his way up a crooked and uncertain stairway in the very heart of Baxter Street, his attention was arrested by hearing a voice (evidently a woman's) in prayer. He was on the landing of the third story of a coloured sailors' boarding-house, and from the surroundings it was the last place on earth one would expect to hear a prayer to the Almighty God. The supplicant was praying away in a manner which showed she was undisturbed by the surroundings, and it was plain to the hearer that she had no doubt at all that she had the ear of the heavenly Father. Unwilling to disturb such a solemn scene, the *Revival* man took off his hat and felt for his pencil.

" ' O Lord,' said the voice, ' how good Thou art. How precious You have been to us. Blessed be Thy dear name forever. We never called on Thee but Thou didst come. Now, dear Saviour, You know all about me. I can never thank You enough for what

You have done for me, but, dear Jesus, stay with me. I am weak, Thou knowest how I have tried to win souls for Thee. Thou knowest all about this neighbourhood. Do, dear Jesus, help me to bring souls to Christ.'

"We cannot give it all here. As soon as there was silence the reporter knocked at the door and found himself in a plain, neatly furnished room. Three women and one man were on their knees at a round table in the centre of it, and the writer hastily uncovered his head and knelt down with them. One verse of a sweet melody was sung and then after all had risen, a kind but determined-looking woman approached the writer to learn the cause of the intrusion. A few words only were necessary to place everyone on a comfortable footing.

"The *Revival* man was in search of the well-known Baxter Street missionary, Mrs. Doolittle, and had got at her very door before he was aware of it. This is one of the most remarkable women in the mission field. She secured a foothold in Baxter Street ten years ago, and bad as the street is now, it is nothing to what it was then. She goes in saloons and preaches Sunday afternoons and uses the bar to lay her Bible and hymn book on. No one touches her, and so great is her influence over this class, that they all would resent an insult towards her. She goes into the lowest brothels and dance houses and openly persuades young girls to leave; if she cannot obtain her point, she prays with them. When asked how she could do this she exclaimed: 'Me? I can't do it. It is all Jesus, bless the Lord!'

"And then warming up with her theme, so her face

fairly shone with rapture, she added: 'Praise the
Lord, praise the Lord! Brother,' said she, 'do you
know we don't praise him half enough.'"

"THE STRONGER OF THE TWO

"The love of whiskey is stronger than the love of
money. It is said the 'love of money is the root of
all evil.' It is the love of money that keeps the world
moving. What will men not do for money? They
will cross the seas, climb over mountains, work in
dark rayless caverns, expose themselves to all sorts of
dangers, deprive themselves of all comforts, endure
fatigues—almost anything within the reach of human
capacity, and then, after having secured it by such
means, they sacrifice it all for whiskey. Slaves of
this appetite will spend their last dime for whiskey,
no matter how much they may be suffering for the
necessaries of life. We have known men while on a
spree, and being refused a drink on credit, to step in
a hallway and take off their shirt and offer it for rum.
'Only one drink,' they say. 'I will die if I don't
get it. I shall die.'"

"THE LOVE FOR WHISKEY

"Men thoroughly under the influence of this appetite are utterly indifferent to the love of home. Not
only are the wants and wishes of loved ones disre-
garded, but their comfort and happiness sacrificed in
order to gratify the unquenchable thirst for strong
drink. There is probably nothing on earth that can
compare with alcohol as a despoiler of home.

"What will a sane man not do to protect and defend

his fireside? What labours, fatigues, privations will he not cheerfully go through with to provide for the wants of those who are dependent upon him; and yet under the influence of this inordinate and depraved appetite, he grows indifferent and neglectful, and even spurns contemptuously the sad pleadings of suffering loved ones. There is nothing under the sun that so thoroughly conquers man's love for his family and friends as the appetite for whiskey or beer. Afflictions, sorrows and disappointments only tend to bind men closer to their home life, but alcohol, that enemy of the home, that despoiler of peace, that breeder of discord, that foe to friendship, that stranger to love, tends to estrange and alienate men from all that is pure, peaceable and lovely."

" THE DECEITFULNESS OF WHISKEY

" One who wielded an inspired pen many hundred years ago, said, speaking of wine: ' Whosoever is deceived thereby is not wise.' There is nothing on earth that deceives us as does the intoxicating drink. It promises to slake thirst, but instead of doing so it creates a deeper thirst. It promises happiness and peace, but instead of these boons it brings misery, confusion and despair. It promises health and long life, but it really brings disease, and a premature and terrible death. Who except those who have passed through it, can tell the suffering and anguish that takes possession of the man or woman who is a slave to rum. The fearful apprehension of something awful that is about to happen, the longing for sleep, and the dread to go to sleep for fear we will wake up in hell. How it deceives us too, that we are not so bad after all, that what we did would be excused because we were drunk. We imagine we are in bad luck. It was not our fault that we were discharged from our job, oh, no; rum will conjure up a hundred excuses, and we go to the fatal cup for comfort. It is almost useless to talk to a man who is so deceived. He must go to the bottom. He must realise that it is not bad luck. It is not bad health or bad friends that have brought all this trouble, but it is whiskey and nothing but whiskey.

"Another style of deception of this foe of mankind is the way it creeps on us unawares. How slowly and stealthily it advances on its unsuspecting victim. Its progress is almost imperceptible. The unfortunate one is not conscious of its approach until he awakes from his deceptive slumber of self-security to find himself bound hand and foot, and with no power to extricate himself from its merciless and unyielding grasp. He writhes and struggles in vain for deliverance. It has entwined its secret forces about every limb, and he lies chained in hopeless bondage to an ungovernable appetite.

"At first, the drunkard is master of his appetite, but it is only for a brief time. He soon becomes its servant, and finally its most loyal and menial slave. In the language of one who tasted the bitterest dregs, 'Alcohol was at first my jolly companion. I soon became its humble and obedient servant, and now I am its helpless and cowardly slave.'

"There is one refuge, thank God. That only refuge is in the Lord Jesus Christ. No one can doubt but that the very devil is in the cup. There is no disguising the demon that goes down your throat with

the whiskey you swallow. All drunkards know that
rum is their mortal foe, so the only course left is to
turn to the friend of all mankind, the dear Saviour,
who stands with loving arms waiting to receive you.
Oh! poor, tired, drunken, weary soul, how much you
need rest. How bad the devil has used you, how
poorly he has paid you. Shake off his bonds and
make one grand glorious effort. Look up to Christ,
and say I will go to Jesus. I'll go to Him though I
die, and who dare hinder me? Dear friend, whenever
you come to this point, you have the victory. Satan
will flee in real alarm, and then just let go and drop.
Christ will catch you; and oh! the rest, the sweet,
sweet rest, that will be yours. Try it."

" THE APPETITE FOR ALCOHOL

" We have heard people claim to have a natural
appetite for whiskey and strong drink; but this is a
great mistake; nature never bred or developed such
a contradiction, such an anomaly. If she had she
would have created alcohol with which to satisfy it,
and this she has not done. It is not found in nature's
laboratory.

" Nature makes ample provisions for all those wants
that are natural, but she made no provisions whatever for the alcoholic appetite, therefore it is unnatural.

" God made man upright and honest, but he has
sought out many inventions and this is one of them.
Appetite is very largely if not wholly an artificial
creature and capable of almost any degree of per-
version.

" When under restraint and controlled by reason and
judgment, it is one of the greatest sources of health

and happiness known to mankind, but when it once gets the mastery over these attributes it becomes a merciless tyrant, enslaving to its menial servitude all the highest and best capacities of soul, body and spirit."

S. H. Hadley was passionately devoted to his mother. I have again and again seen the tears glisten in his eyes as he told the story of her devotion to him, and of the expectation he had of one day being with her again. The editorial which follows is but another indication of this.

" MOTHER

" What a world of memories cluster round that word. How we each begin to think of our own dear mother. Our recollections go back to childhood, when we first become acquainted with that dear, sweet face. About the first thing we can remember of her is as we knelt down at her side and said the prayers she taught us. Then she would lift us up so tenderly and put us to bed, and tuck us in and give us a good hug and a good-night kiss. When we were sick, how she would stand over us with that anxious look, never weary, never tired, and when we would go to sleep and awake mother was always there, wide-awake. Indeed, we often used to wonder in our childhood innocence when mother did sleep. The first face we shall look for when we get to heaven, and the first one we expect to see, will be mother's; and we expect her sweet, gentle voice to be the first sound that will break with rapture on our ears. When she was sick we would steal into the room on tip-toe, with a great fear in our heart. A dread of, we did not know what, and a choking sensation at the throat; we did not intend to speak to her; but mother heard us, no matter how softly we stepped, and turned her dear face over and we climbed up on a chair for a kiss.

" But the time rolled on and we grew up to be a large boy. We came to the conclusion that mothers were excellent when we were little, but got somewhat troublesome when a boy was trying to be a man. How horrified she was when she first smelt tobacco-smoke on us, and can we ever forget how the look of anxiety turned to real anguish when she detected liquor on our breath. At last the time came when she could only pray. She would pour out her soul in prayer to Him who bore all our sorrows. What a blessed thing there is a place where mother can go, when her very heart seems to be breaking in agony. Before we got to be so careless and hardened, we sometimes had moments of remorse, and conscience would prick us for causing our dear mother so much sorrow, and then how quickly she forgave us, and with her arms around us kissed us with the old confidence restored. But, alas! these spells would be of short duration, and rum had already begun to do its work. Then the lines would begin to grow deep on that face that was so peaceful, and tear-stains were often found there. All this time we loved our mother, and we knew she was the best friend we had on earth; but the deadly poisonous serpent we were taking stilled the voice and pleadings of mother, as well as all other holy things.

" At last when we came home late one night some-one met us at the door. It wasn't mother,—it was some kind friend, and we are told 'mother is

dead.' 'What, mother dead?' The first face we ever
saw pale and cold. The first voice we ever heard
hushed in the awful stillness of death. It must be
a mistake; but at the same time something in the
very stillness told us she was dead. We thought as
we approached the house a few moments ago that
we would not have her see us for anything; but now
we would be willing our whole life should be laid
bare if she could only speak to us once more and bid
us good-bye, ere she took that eternal sleep. 'Will
you go to see her now?' was asked. 'Yes,' we
would go. We did not know what else to say. We
followed along to the chamber of death. Oh! dear,
could that be mother! That rigid form with a white
sheet so carefully laid over it. They lifted the cloth
off, and we saw it was her indeed. It was no horrid
dream, as we had hoped. Then we looked so closely,
to see if we could find any traces of anger or reproof
or displeasure; for it was then we knew it would be
for us; but it was not there. Before her soul had
taken its flight she had been permitted mayhap to
catch a glimpse of the Eternal City beyond, and it
wore a peaceful, sweet look. 'Did she say anything
about me? Did she leave me any word?' we asked
with choking voice. 'Oh, yes! she told us to tell
you that she had prayed for you, so many times, and
she knew God would bring in her dear wandering
boy, and he must be sure and meet her in heaven.'

"Yes, indeed, we would! Ah, yes! We almost
wished we could die then, and go to her. And as we
stood there in awe looking upon the work that death
had wrought, we remembered the song we had learned
in childhood:

"'Mother, thou wast mild and lovely,
Gentle as the summer breeze,
Pleasant as the air of evening,
When it floats among the trees.'

" In after years when sin and vice, and rum, had us firmly in their toils, we would sometimes call to mind that dear dead face and remember those prayers of mother's, and then we would go and drink deeper, and try, though in vain, to drown all these thoughts. But a mother's prayer will never die. The fervent agonising prayer of a true Christian mother will go up to God, and it will be answered some day in God's own time. It will never fall to the ground. We know God heard it, in our behalf."

" OH, RUMSELLER!

" I would not take your death for all this life affords, and all its multiplied pleasures. Oh, thou corrupter of youth, and disseminator of misery and woe, and tears and sobs. When you draw near to death, how will it be? To the Christian these shadows are tinted with a golden hue, and the heaven's light shines through and over it. But to you these shall be shadows full of demons. Images of terror shall dimly rise and beckon you on. The ghostly deeds of the past shall arise and stretch out their skinny hands to push you forward. You will not die unattended. No, indeed. There will be plenty of company around your bedside. Despair will mock you. Agony shall press to your parched lips her fiery cup. Remorse will feel for your heart and rend it open. Good men will breathe the freer when you are dead, and utter thanksgiving when you are gone, and feel as though a plague is stayed, and surrounded by fiends, and borne on a blast, your guilty spirit whistles toward the city of death and night, and the shrieks of those who have been damned through the liquor you have sold them will be your first welcome to the place where you will send up your unavailing and helpless cry throughout a never-ending eternity.

"Poor soul. He don't seem to realise that he will die if he does get it. If these poor unfortunate rum and sin-cursed souls will only come to some of the missions, whose hospitable doors are ever open to receive them, and give their hearts to God and ask His help, they would soon learn the only true way to overcome the greatest of all curses,—rum."

It was from this experience that his great mission to the outcast started. I have often heard him say that when he reached the Cremorne Mission the room was crowded and the crowd reached out into the street, but an old man said to him, "Do you want to go in?" Tremblingly he replied, "I do if I can." "Well," said he, "just take hold of my coat-tails and follow me." Holding on for dear life like as a drowning man would catch at a rope, he was drawn through the crowd until he stood near the front. His conversion was the result and his marvellous mission is begun.

The name of the aged man has never been known, but doubtless he is to-day in glory, and if so, S. H. Hadley must have met him, and they two rejoice together over the mighty work accomplished by this truly wonderful man.

XV

SOME PERSONAL TESTIMONIES

AN entire volume could be written embracing the personal testimonies of the devotion in which S. H. Hadley was held, not only by his friends, but by the outcast men and women who had no claim upon him at all, except that Jesus loved them, and he loved Jesus. His eye always seemed to be open for the one who was down and out. He would pass by a man of affairs to take the hand of a reeling, staggering drunkard, but it is a pleasure to record not only the testimonies of men who were redeemed like himself, but of some men of renown.

"A PERSONAL APPRECIATION

By Rev. R. A. Torrey, D. D.

" I regard the late Samuel H. Hadley as one of the most beautiful characters I have ever met. He was the embodiment of Christlike love. I think I have never heard any man who made me feel the short-comings in my life, in my lack of love for the outcast as he did. One address that I heard him give on love for the lost has moulded my whole life since. He was a daily demonstration of the power of Christ to save. While I admired him, I did not so much admire him as love him. I have met very few men in all my life to whom my heart went out as it did to Samuel Hadley." THE WESTMINSTER.

By the Rev. J. Wesley Johnston.

" Among the varied experiences which have be-
fallen me since entering the ministry, there is none that
I value more or that has been more significant in
results, than my pastoral relations with Rev. S. H.
Hadley, who for so many years was the superintendent of the far-famed McAuley Mission on Water
Street, and the superintendent of our rescue mission
on the Bowery. For through this relation I have
been enabled to reach certain religious convictions and
attain certain spiritual phases, to which I had hitherto
been a comparative stranger. For though I was his
pastor in the largest meaning of that suggestive term
—enjoying his confidence, sharing his hopes, bearing
something of his burdens, and favoured as few men
have been with the secret desires of his soul—yet in
reality he was my pastor, for everything that I was
to him, he was to me, except that his sympathies were
deeper, his love richer, his wisdom sounder, and his
care more fatherly and protective. Only those who
have stood in this relation to him can realise what
it means to have such a man in his church, or feel
the awful sense of desolation when such a man is
taken away.

" My acquaintance with Mr. Hadley began when
I was pastor of the Sixty-first Street church in this
city, for he came to see me and talked freely of the
work in the McAuley Mission. Some years later
when I was stationed in St. John's Church, Brooklyn,
I visited the McAuley Mission, and saw for myself
the wonderful work that mission was doing. But

it was not until I was appointed to John Street church, in which Mr. Hadley held his membership, that I came to know him with any measure of intimacy, or appreciate in even the slightest degree his extraordinary ability and power. And what was true of me five years ago is true of multitudes now. Because he identified himself so closely with the McAuley Mission, living for all these years in Water Street, mingling constantly with drunkards, criminals, outcasts, and sinners of every class, visiting squalid lodging houses and sinful resorts, going everywhere that he might find those who needed help, many have imagined that by nature he was fitted for just this service and had neither taste nor aptitude for anything else. On the contrary, Mr. Hadley was a man of the most exquisite refinement. Vulgarity in any form was impossible to him. He had a keen sense of the proprieties. His bearing, whether in the intimacy of private friendship or public life, was of the highest type, and any remark or experience which savoured of coarseness called from him an indignant rebuke. A more noble Christian gentleman it would be difficult to find.

" It would be only natural to suppose that coming constantly in contact with those who frequented the missions that he would in some measure become familiar with vice, and lose his fine delicacy and sense of feeling. For that seems almost an inevitable result. The tendency of repetition is to harden. By seeing suffering every day the eye loses its tenderness and the heart grows indifferent. But who ever saw either hardness or indifference with Mr. Hadley? Who ever heard a rough or unfeeling word from his

lips? Who ever knew of him turning coldly or neg-
lectfully away from even the most vicious and degraded? He was the embodiment of chivalry to lost
women. He was the soul of kindness to dissolute men.
His smile, though tear-shot, was that of a mother when
wayward girls wandered into the Mission from the
streets. His hand, though trembling with emotion,
was that of a father when the weary, repentant prodi-
gal came forward to the mourners' bench. How he
kept so sweet, so patient, so tender, so pitiful can never
be explained, for the secret lay between him and God.
But it must have cost him nights of prayer, days of
anguish, times of unutterable sorrow. Yet no matter
what it cost it yielded a splendid return, for it can be
said of him as of the Master whom he ardently loved,
' He was touched with the feeling of our infirmities.'

"But there was one phase of Mr. Hadley's work
concerning which comparatively little has been said,
yet it is of supreme importance—his close relation and
intense sympathy with the church.

"As a rule men who lead off in reforms, whether
social or philanthropic, rarely identify themselves defi-
nitely with the church. For some reason, possibly
because they think the church is failing in its duty, or
is not keenly alive to the cause dear to their hearts,
they are often open in their denouncement, and at
times seem frankly hostile to both churches and ministers. Hence it is not unusual to hear of the exclusive-
ness of the church; the pride, the formality, the
indifference of the church; the carelessness of the
church with regard to the condition of the outcast
and the poor; and the chill welcome the church has
for those who are not of the prosperous and favoured

class. Indeed, it is more than probable that much of the present feeling of distinction between the rich and the poor, and the supposed failure of the church to reach the great masses of the working people is fostered by these so-called reformers who have made the church the target for foolish and harmful criticism.

"But Mr. Hadley took exactly the opposite course. The Mission on Water Street and the Rescue Hall on the Bowery were not regarded by him as separate institutions to which men might come because they would not be received elsewhere, but merely as doorways leading into the great church of Christ. Hence with an insistence which was evident at every service he made it very clear that no reform in personal habits, no abandonment of drunkenness, no promise or pledge of amendment was complete unless the vows for such reform were sealed before the altars of the church.

"No man for half a century has done so much to bring the poor and outcast into close vital relations to the church as Mr. Hadley. There is not a church in this city, or in this country, but is under profound obligations to him for the service he has rendered. Had he so desired, with the immense following he had throughout the nation, and with his extraordinary gifts of speech and his power to awaken popular sympathy, he could easily have founded a Rescue Mission Church, and thus created a feeling that the church generally cared nothing for the wayward, the drunken or the poor. But his love for the church and his splendid faith in the gospel it proclaimed, led him to cast the entire weight of his influence and the force of his personality to the church of Christ, and he contended boldly that any pledge or promise, no matter how solemnly it was made, was only as a house built upon the sand, unless it centred itself in the Gospel and church of our blessed Lord.

" In connection with this it needs to be said that while he was most desirous that the Mission converts unite with the church, he made it very clear to them that a change, a definite change of life and heart, was essential. The mere fact of raising the hand for prayers or coming forward to the seekers' bench and there professing conversion, did not in his mind fit a man for church membership. He looked for and required an intelligent faith, not simply in the Gospel, which is often an unmeaning phrase, but in Jesus as a distinct personal Saviour.

" To Mr. Hadley, Jesus was not a mere name enshrined in a creed, a vague, mysterious being, throned above principalities and powers, beyond the reach of sinful men, but an actual person, who came into his life with a vividness akin to that of a bodily presence, and whose absolute existence was as positive as that of his own.

" And if anyone is looking for the secret of Mr. Hadley's wonderful success, the source of his unfailing sympathy, the cause of his deep, forgiving grace, which not even the seventy times seven could exhaust, or the inspiration of his ceaseless, tireless ministry, it all can be summed up in the fact that his religion was not a creed, not a catechism, not a summary of Christian doctrines, not an observance of church duties, but a firm realisation of Christ as a person, with whom he had conscious communion, and from whom he received blessings as clearly as from the hand of a friend.

"Yet there was not the slightest tinge of fanaticism in his religious life. He was singularly well poised, steady, calm, strong in all matters pertaining to religion. Seeing what he saw most every day; hearing the testimonies of multitudes of men who through his ministry had been gloriously converted; living in an atmosphere of constant revival, it would not have been surprising if in time something of extravagance, unwise excitement, tendencies towards mysticism, had been apparent.

"But instead of being elated by his success, or affected by the popularity he attained, he became increasingly humble, and his utter dependence upon God was daily more manifest.

"And this spirit he sought with all earnestness to impress upon the Mission converts. Their help, their only help, he insisted, was God. Anything else would fail them. They must pray. They must read their Bibles. They must maintain constant communion with Jesus. They must be deeply religious. They must rest with absolute faith on the promises of God. If they trusted in God, their old appetites, lusts, desires, temptations, no matter how powerful in the old life, would not longer have dominion over them. In this way he made religion a real thing. He had no place for theories in his Mission. God, heaven, hell, sin, Christ, salvation, the power of prayer, the indwelling of the Holy Spirit, grace for even the most abandoned and degraded, were tremendous verities with him, and he made them the essentials of his ministry. No wonder, therefore, that so many of his converts remain faithful. He made religion to them as real as it was to himself. He brought them face to face with Jesus as a personal Saviour, through whom alone they could obtain salvation.

" Now the service he thus rendered to the cause of religion is simply incalculable. He brought men back to the faith and earnestness of primitive Christianity. He wrote anew the Acts of the Apostles. He transferred the Upper Room, with its strange manifestations of the power of God, from the Jerusalem of two millenniums ago, to the mission chapel on Water Street, or the Rescue Hall on the Bowery. The miracles of Jesus he wrought out in flesh and blood. He had no doubts, no fears, no misgivings concerning the faith once delivered to the saints. He could say just as earnestly as St. Peter, ' We have not followed cunningly devised fables, when we made known unto you the power and coming of our Lord Jesus Christ, but were eye-witnesses of His majesty.' Not even St. Paul, when standing before Agrippa, could relate with more startling vividness the story of his conversion than he could tell of the wondrous night when Jesus appeared to him and gave him the assurance of sins forgiven. He needed neither argument nor evidence to convince him as to the reality of miracles, for he had the witness in himself. And his life gave glorious proof of what he declared, for it was blameless, pure, upright, honest, consecrated to the saving of his fellow-men, and like that of the Christ who had appeared to him, spent ministering to the poor, caring for the outcasts and redeeming the lost from the bondage of sin and death.

" Thank God for such a man, such a ministry, such

a life! Thank God for such a work as he was able to do, and for such a record as he has left behind! But surely such a work cannot stop now. Never was the call so loud or the need so urgent. There are multitudes in the valley, not of decision, but of crime, poverty, shame, drunkenness, despair. And they cannot save themselves. The chains of habit are upon them. The fetters of appetite bind them. The prisons of despair enclose them. The memories of sin haunt them. We do well then to pray that God will raise up other men of the same type as Samuel H. Hadley —gracious, tender, winning, loving—and thus carry on the work to which Jesus gave himself—seeking and saving the lost."

Mr. Hadley was frequently invited to speak to students. Among the invitations he prized most highly was one that came to him almost annually during the last years of his life to address the professors and students of the University of Pennsylvania. While on one of these visits he was invited to speak at the Garrick Theatre, and concerning this meeting the following was written:

" A REPORTER'S APPRECIATION

By William T. Ellis

" S. H. Hadley, known to the Bowery and the underworld generally as ' Hopp ' Hadley, superintendent of the old Jerry McAuley Mission, New York, to the reading public as the author of a recent unique volume, alive with human interest, ' Down in Water Street,' and to church folks generally as the country's foremost exponent of religious work for outcasts, addressed a Philadelphia audience yesterday noon in the Garrick Theatre, under the auspices of the Interdenominational Committee for Work outside of the Churches, which is holding a series of noon theatre meetings for business people on Thursday, a series for workingmen on Sunday afternoons in the Grand Opera House, and another for students on Sunday evenings in the Garrick. To this last named meeting Mr. Hadley will speak next Sunday night.

" Mr. Hadley does not look like a preacher. No street urchin ever yelled ' dude ' after him, either. Until he smiles he might pass as one of the better grade of the members of Tammany Hall; but the smile shows him a saint, and Tammany Hall has no niche for saints. When he speaks he displays the New York tag, which twenty years' residence on the Bowery has engraved rather more deeply than ordinary. There is no imminent danger of his ever being called to a professorship of rhetoric in what he disdainfully described as ' A Tom Paine Club, a Theological Cemetery.' There is a breezy colloquialism and unconventionality about the man which, joined to his intense earnestness, won for him a rapt attention from yesterday's audience, such as more polished speakers do not often secure.

" A WAY THEY HAVE ON THE BOWERY

" When half way through the Scripture lesson, a portion of the Sermon on the Mount, Mr. Hadley stopped to illustrate the passage, ' Him that taketh away thy cloak forbid not to take thy coat also,' by a story of an ex-convict and drunkard to whom had been given work in Water Street Mission and who promptly stole the superintendent's overcoat. After the resulting spree and arrest were over the man returned. 'After every other place kicks them out, even the gin mills and the penitentiaries, for we take those whom the devil himself doesn't want, they come back to Water Street—and he was restored to his former position. Again he stole another overcoat. Again he came back when out of jail and was forgiven; and it was that mercy which broke his heart and made a man of him.' Then Mr. Hadley announced his text as, 'He is kind unto the unthankful and to the evil,' saying, 'I know most of that kind of Gospel.'

"WHY HE BELIEVED HIM THE DEVIL

"The address was far from being a sermon. It was the recital of one man's life story, a man who commenced 'with the best drinks that could be had and ended in the gutter, and for some years before my conversion could not get a nickel without stealing it,' and who had committed one hundred and twenty-five forgeries on one man alone—an outcast from friends, family, respectability and honesty, a habitue of the lowest gin mills. 'A theological professor once asked me, "Do you believe in a devil?" I said, "Sure! I've seen him and walked with him and lived with him."'

"It was in the old Jerry McAuley Cremorne Mission that Mr. Hadley himself was converted, twenty-two years ago. He had had himself locked up for several days, that he might be out of the reach of

drink. 'My first prayer was in a police station, and
I've been back in that cell just twenty-two times since
to tell the Lord what I think of Him.' When released he went down to the Mission, and met Jerry
McAuley, 'The Apostle to the Drunkard.'

"For nineteen years Mr. Hadley himself has been
superintendent of the Mission. 'Our constituency is
made up of lost men. The churches have got through
with them, the gin mills have kicked them out. Our
Mission is the lowest downtown. When you get down
to Water Street, you cannot get any lower.'

"MIRACLES ON WATER STREET

"Describing the work of the Mission Mr. Hadley
told a number of stories. One was of Phil McGuire,
who before entering the mission had 'pawned his
shirt for ten cents, the price of two drinks of Fourth
Ward whiskey. I saw that old bum transformed, instantly, from a thief, a drunkard and a liar, into a
clean-hearted, upright man, who for years thereafter
lived and worked in the Mission, right in my family.
I never saw a man more careful and just in money
matters. His last act before he died was to make sure
he had accounted for some money he held. At his
funeral there was such a crowd of those who loved
him that the house could not hold them and I had to
lock the door—millionaires, drunks, preachers, thieves,
noble women and girls of the street, redeemed men
whom he had helped, all crowded together—Water
Street had not seen such a sight for years. That's
what the Gospel is doing.'"

XVI

THE FUNERAL SERVICES AT WATER STREET MISSION

ONE of the most remarkable funerals ever held in the city of New York was that of Mr. Hadley at the Water Street Mission, the scene of his victorious life.

There were present great men of affairs and poor wrecks of humanity who had lost everything and had passed through the door of the Mission just for the privilege of looking again upon the face that had always looked with love into their own wretched, sinful hearts.

There were prominent ministers, great evangelists, society ladies, as well as women who had belonged to the under world in other days, but all were there for a single purpose, namely, to pay a tribute to the memory of a dearly loved friend.

From the beginning to the end there was not one mournful note struck in the service. It was just such an occasion as he himself would have been pleased with.

The singing was true Water Street singing and the addresses were all delivered in a triumphant tone of voice, showing that the Christian hope of a glorious resurrection had gripped every speaker.

Mr. Walter M. Smith, one of the Trustees, and one of the best friends the Mission ever had, as well as a most devoted friend of Mr. Hadley, presided at the services. Without the least formality he rose and said:

" While we are waiting for the family to come I am going to ask Mr. Alexander to lead us in the ' Glory Song.' " With this simple announcement Mr. Charles M. Alexander, who has sung his way around the world and into the hearts of a countless multitude of Christians everywhere, the most remarkable leader of evangelistic music in the world to-day, stood up, brushed away the tears from his eyes, did his very best to control his emotions and then said: " Friends, my heart is so full this morning that I cannot sing; I am going to ask Mr. Butler, who is with me, to sing the verses of the Glory Song and we will all sing the chorus." Mr. Charles Butler responded at once and the famous Glory Song, not only the verses under the matchless singing of Mr. Butler, but also the chorus, thrilled us all. It was wonderful to hear the people sing:

> " When all my labours and trials are o'er,
> And I am safe on that beautiful shore,
> Just to be near the dear Lord I adore,
> Will thro' the ages be glory for me.

> " When by the gift of his infinite grace,
> I am accorded in heaven a place,
> Just to be there and to look on His face,
> Will thro' the ages be glory for me.

> " Friends will be there I have loved long ago;
> Joy like a river around me will flow;
> Yet just a smile from my Saviour, I know,
> Will thro' the ages be glory for me.

"Oh, that will be glory for me,
Glory for me, glory for me,
When by His grace I shall look on His face,
That will be glory, be glory for me."

One of Mr. Hadley's favourite songs was an adaptation of words to the music of "Old Black Joe." A quartet of his friends rendered this selection with most telling effect. At Mr. Smith's request Dr. J. Wilbur Chapman offered the invocation.

Miss Bertha Irene Chapman sang "The Name of Jesus." It was one of Mr. Hadley's favourite songs and she had often sung it for him.

Mr. Walter M. Smith said: "Dear friends, I have been told by our dear brother, and he has also told it in his book, that when he was first called to preside as superintendent of this Mission, after long days of prayer on the part of himself and his dear wife, they selected the fifty-eighth chapter of Isaiah, from the third to the twelfth verses, as an answer to their prayer; and it seems to me that nothing out of the sacred Word could be more appropriate than to again read that lesson, and I am going to ask the Rev. Dr. Pierson to do this for us."

Dr. A. T. Pierson said: "Before I read, let me say with reference to that hymn which has just been sung that I never heard a man speak the name of Jesus as Samuel Hadley did. It has had new music in it ever since I heard him say it; I never knew a man that threw so much heart into the pronunciation of the name of Jesus as Hadley did." Dr. Pierson then read the portion of Scripture, which is as follows:

"Wherefore have we fasted, say they, and thou seest not? wherefore have we afflicted our soul, and thou takest no knowledge? Behold, in the day of your fast ye find pleasure, and exact all your labours. Behold, ye fast for strife and debate, and to smite with the fist of wickedness; ye shall not fast as ye do this day, to make your voice to be heard on high.

"Is it such a fast that I have chosen? a day for a man to afflict his soul? is it to bow down his head as a bulrush, and to spread sackcloth and ashes under him? wilt thou call this a fast, and an acceptable day to the Lord?

"Is not this the fast that I have chosen? to loose the bands of wickedness, to undo the heavy burdens, and to let the oppressed go free, and that ye break every yoke?

"Is it not to deal thy bread to the hungry, and that thou bring the poor that are cast out to thy house? when thou seest the naked, that thou cover him; and that thou hide not thyself from thine own flesh?

"Then shall thy light break forth as the morning, and thine health shall spring forth speedily; and thy righteousness shall go before thee; the glory of the Lord shall be thy reward.

"Then shall thou call, and the Lord shall answer; thou shalt cry and he will say, Here I am. If thou take away from the midst of thee the yoke, the putting forth of the finger, and speaking vanity;

"And if thou draw out thy soul to the hungry, and satisfy the afflicted soul; then shall thy light rise in obscurity, and thy darkness be as the noon day.

"And the Lord shall guide thee continually, and satisfy thy soul in drought, and make fat thy bones;

and thou shalt be like a watered garden, and like a spring of water, whose waters fail not.

"And they that shall be of thee shall build the old waste places; thou shalt raise up the foundations of many generations; and thou shall be called, The repairer of the breach, The Restorer of paths to dwell in" (ISAIAH lviii. 3-12).

Mr. Walter M. Smith said: "Our dear friend has told us that, upon the occasion of his first meeting as superintendent of this Mission before he came downstairs, he looked down through yonder window at the gathering throng and felt appalled, and he said he felt abashed. So he went back into the little room at the side of the window, which he occupied as his office, and falling down on his knees he asked the Lord to give him a token, and that the token might be one soul. He said the reason he didn't ask for a score was perhaps that he hadn't faith enough to ask for more. But he did ask for one; and when he gave the invitation, a single hand was uplifted, and a single soul came forward and was saved, and that soul, dear friends, in the shape of a mortal man is here before us; and I think nothing could be more appropriate on this occasion than to ask Mr. James C. Edwards to give us his testimony as that saved man."

Standing beside the casket Mr. Edwards said: "Friends, I don't know what to say. I feel to-day that I have lost not only a friend, but a brother. Nineteen years and nine months and eleven days and eleven nights ago I came staggering into those doors there, a homeless, lost drunkard. I had been a drunkard from my boyhood. I stood 'way down by the door there, drunk. I don't remember what Brother Hadley said, or what prayers were prayed, but I know this much, that I got up here somehow to the front and one dear soul came to me and knelt down beside me. I mean Mrs. Hadley, God bless her. That night when I got off my knees the desire for rum and everything else evil had gone out of me. I went down on my knees drunk, but God saved me sober, and the best part of it is I have been sober ever since. I am not a bum, not a tramp on the streets of New York; my employer, who is sitting on the platform, can tell you what I have been since then. It is only the grace of God that did it.

" I recall that when Brother Hadley was putting up the tablet over there to the memory of Jerry McAuley he was in doubt about what text to put at the bottom of the inscription, but finally decided on ' He resteth from his labours and his works do follow him.' That is just what Brother Hadley is doing to-day, resting from his labours, and his works will follow him. I know that thousands upon thousands will miss S. H. Hadley, even if it is for nothing else than the kind word he used to give, and the warm ' God bless you! ' and shake of the hand. I ask you, friends, to pray for me and for the rest of us in this hall to-day."

Mr. W. M. Smith said: " Friends, one whom I know to have been very close to our brother, and who was present and presided at the meeting to which I have referred, was Mr. R. Fulton Cutting, and I am sure we would be glad to hear a few words from him."

Mr. R. Fulton Cutting said: " This hardly seems to be the time for many words. It is true I have known Mr. Hadley since he first took charge of the work. When he first came in there were a few good people who distrusted him; it made it pretty hard for him at first, as it always does for a man who is sincerely trying to do the best he can. But he replied with the only unanswerable reply, a life of consistent consecration. He knew there was One who trusted him all the time; One who perfectly understood him, to whom he could tell his whole heart. But Hadley found a great many men in his after life who had confidence in him, who would trust him perhaps next to their God, because they knew him. He was one of those genuine men. He spoke his mind right straight out.

"Another characteristic of Hadley's was his intensely shrewd common sense. He was a deeply emotional man, as we all know, but his emotion never carried him beyond the limits of solid common sense. There is such a thing as zeal without knowledge; it's a great deal better than knowledge without zeal, but still we do make mistakes sometimes in the excess of emotionalism. Hadley rarely made them. A man of the most abiding optimism, he trusted all that came near him to such a degree that he conveyed his optimism to them and made them trust themselves when nothing else outside the power of God could have done. He used his mind as well as his heart down here.

"Now let us see whether we cannot make his memory a living thing to every one of us, to go with us all through the rest of our lives; practise something of his genuineness, his common sense, but above all his entire and single-hearted consecration to his Master. We will honour him by so doing as we never could honour him in any other way. We can build monuments, pass all kinds of resolutions, and do all sorts of things, but the monument he would like us to set up is a monument in our own hearts, the influence of which shall pass out from our hearts into the lives of others, and make itself to a certain degree the re-embodiment of his devoted spirit, to go out and try to do what he did for others."

Mr. W. M. Smith next asked the Trustees of the Mission to say a few words in appreciation of Mr. Hadley's life and work.

Mr. W. T. Wardwell said: "Dear friends, I feel like my Brother Alexander, the singer: I can't speak to-day. Whatever I say I say with a sob in my voice, and I only want to say that I loved Brother Hadley with all my heart, I trusted him with all my heart, I believed in him with my whole soul. Yesterday when I was thinking about his death, wondering why he should have been taken away, and trying in a dim way to understand just what the reason might be, the thought came into my mind, perhaps after all the Lord wanted him and He has said to him, 'You have worked long enough for Me, Hadley, come up to your reward.' And I couldn't help thinking what a joyous time he must have had with all those who have gone up from this room and with all the friends he had in this city."

Mr. W. E. Lougee said: "It has been said by one of our silver-tongued orators that from time immemorial it has been a beautiful custom to mingle with our mourning for the dead eulogy for their well-spent lives. Eulogies are not needed in the presence of this gathering to-day for our dear Brother Hadley. His life speaks of what he did far more loudly than words could tell. There were characteristics in his life that made it a benediction and a blessing to us who came in contact with him on business lines as well as the saving of men. That consuming passion for lost men was shown all his life. 'Lord, spare my life a little longer that I may patch up a few more souls.' Not for his home or family; not for any other work; but for lost men, for whom he had given his life. 'Spare me that I may patch up a few more broken lives.'

" Our Master was once approached by His disciples and asked, 'How often shall we forgive a man, until seven times?' Jesus looked at them with that wonderful compassion that shone out of His eyes in His love for lost men and said, 'Not until seven times, but until seventy times seven.' And that was Hadley's life, helping a man when human patience would have been all gone; you and I wouldn't have been patient with them as our Lord and Hadley were. But He loved them, and He had patience with them, He bound up their wounds. And that was Hadley's life, and that is the life that appeals to us. Is it worth much? I tell you, as we think of the life that Hadley led these nineteen years, and of the lives he has touched, doesn't it inspire you to a deeper consecration, a deeper longing for lost men, so that when you come to lie where our friend Hadley lies you may, as he, be loved and honoured of all and accepted by the Master whom he served? "

Mr. S. W. Bowne said: " Dear friends, I am very glad to add my tribute to Brother Hadley on this occasion. When I heard that he had gone to his reward I felt that something had gone out of my life;

I felt a loss such as I have rarely felt even among the
dearest of friends and relatives. He has been a great
blessing to me for a number of years. He has been
an inspiration to my life. He has made me a better
man. And I feel to-day a great personal grief at
Brother Hadley's passing away. He was a dear man,
a magnificent man, a man in every sense of the word,
and with it all, as Brother Cutting has said, a man of
great common sense.

"I remember when we talked of our Mission in the
Bowery, after looking over the ground I rather de-
precated going there, but he didn't agree with me.
He said, 'No, we'll fill this place.' He was right,
and I was wrong; the place was filled, and they are
doing a great work at the Bowery as well as here, as
many of us know. When he would come into my
office for an appeal I never thought for a moment of
refusing what he asked, because I knew it was the
best thing I could do. Friends, we have met with a
great loss. I hope the Lord will raise up someone to
take his place. We can't expect another Hadley to
fill his place, but may we have some strong man to
carry on the Lord's work."

Mr. John S. Huyler said: "Dear friends, I with
the rest of you feel our great loss. I shall always remember our Brother Hadley with great affection, but
especially for the fact that he has taught me the simplicity of the religion of our Lord Jesus Christ. I
remember one night we were in Northfield, and he
was going through the halls singing 'You ask what
makes me happy,' and it was beautiful to hear his
voice. And then we got down to say our prayers before going to bed, and he said, 'Dear Lord, we thank

Thee for the change that can come into a man's life. Here we are to-day, surrounded by friends, everything is pleasant. And this is Thy service. How well I remember that when in the service of the devil I wanted two cents to go across the ferry and couldn't get it!' It was that simplicity of his love and his realisation of what the Master can do that has always been so helpful to us. I had the pleasure of being with him for about six weeks, day and night; we ate together, we slept in the same place; and wherever he was he was always on the hunt for souls. I remember that at the Grand Canyon at Colorado Hadley was very much impressed at the beauty of the scene, and we were all lost in admiration at it. But still Hadley found one other thing there that we didn't find. I happened to look out of the car window, and there stood Hadley with two Indians, their two hands one upon the other, and on the top of that was his little Bible; their hats were off, and he was raising his heart to his Jesus for those poor Indians who had never known anything of Him. God bless the memory of our brother."

Mr. W. M. Smith said: " I have a very dear friend at my side who first introduced me to Brother Hadley and I don't think we would be quite satisfied unless we heard a few words from him who, while never connected officially with the Mission, has always been its firm supporter, Mr. R. L. Cutter.

Mr. Cutter said: " Dear friends, it is needless for me to say how deeply I mourn the loss of this beloved man, but his loss to me is gain to him. When our blessed Lord was here the Pharisees addressed Him in terms of reproach as ' a friend of publicans and sinners.' I thank God He was such a friend, for He became my friend and Saviour, and I am trusting Him. And Hadley on the same lines was a friend of sinners. Oh, what would he not do to bring the Gospel of Jesus to a poor, lost, low-down, suffering man or woman. We all know that tender love, the quality of love which Jesus had, and which I have never seen equalled in any other life I have ever met. God bless to us this service of memorial and of love, for I know it is, and may we all be permitted, through the salvation of Jesus which He has perfected for every man and woman in this room if we will but accept Him, to come at last into that glory where our friend now is."

Mr. W. M. Smith said: "There are probably two hundred people in this room, that would be glad to testify of their real love for our dear brother, and to the saving and keeping power of our Lord and Saviour Jesus Christ. It is manifestly impossible for us to hear from all, but it seems to me, dear friends, that we can stand on our feet, and, in mute eloquence, bow our heads for a minute or two and ask God to bless this meeting and bless every soul in His presence. What more can I say? I can only say this one thing. I want this demonstration from the congregation, that they love and revere His name and that they will consecrate themselves anew to His service, that they will put their arms of love around those who labour for Him, and that this Mission will go on and on and on as long as the world exists and dying men need salvation. Let us all rise, and bow our heads in silent prayer, after which one of our trustees, Hon. M. Linn Bruce, Lieutenant-Governor of New York State will lead us."

Lieutenant-Governor Bruce prayed as follows: " Blessed Saviour, standing in the place where Thy servant laboured for Thee for so many years, help each one of us to consecrate ourselves anew to Thy service. Help us not to weep for him who is with Thee to-day, but give us a consciousness of the responsibility that rests upon us in the added service which Thou wilt require of us in that he is gone; and may each one here bow the knee and the heart and the life to Thy service, to the service of Thee, Oh blessed Christ, for whom he gave his life, his energies, of body, mind and heart; and may this great and glorious work here which he has carried on here for the salvation of men be carried on by those who remain. Wilt Thou help those who are near and dear to him, whose hearts are saddened to-day with the comfort which Thou alone canst give, and which the world cannot take away; may they feel and know that he is with Thee, awaiting their coming; and may each one of us day by day live nearer and closer to Thee in the hope of that glorious immortality which shall come through Thee when Thou shalt call us home. We ask it for Christ's sake."

Mr. W. M. Smith said: " Some of you may expect a word from me about the last illness of our brother. I visited him several times at the hospital, and I want to give you one or two messages. Others have said how near he has been to them. I don't think there is a soul in this room outside of his family that cherished his friendship and love more dearly than I did. He visited my family two weeks ago last Saturday, and he spoke twice on Sunday, in the afternoon to a congregation of men and in the evening to a congregation of young people. I never heard him give his testimony with so much fervour and with such marvellous eloquence. It seemed almost as though the shadow of his approaching death was upon him. We came to New York on the Monday morning, and he complained a little of pain; he said he thought he had an attack of his old trouble. I advised him to go up and see the doctor. He thought perhaps he would. But on Tuesday he came up to our store, and had a short talk with Mr. Cutter and myself. He said to us as he left, ' I won't ask you for another cent again this year.' How prophetic those words were. I saw him, as I have said, in the hospital. He seemed very glad to see me, and inquired after me when I left. I went into his room with Mr. Huyler. He was loath to have an operation performed, as he was afraid his heart wouldn't stand the shock; the surgeons, however, insisted it was the only thing to do and that without it he would not live five hours. He said to Mr. Huyler, ' Living or dying, I am the Lord's,' and I love to think of that as the last expression of his heart and soul. His mind wandered a little after that, and whenever it did wander he always spoke of Water Street. He had a regular Water Street service in that little room all by himself and his Lord; he prayed, he sang, he gave the invitation just the same as he had always done, and apparently he was perfectly happy in doing it. I don't know that I ought to bring a personal matter in here, but somehow or other my heart compels me to do it. He

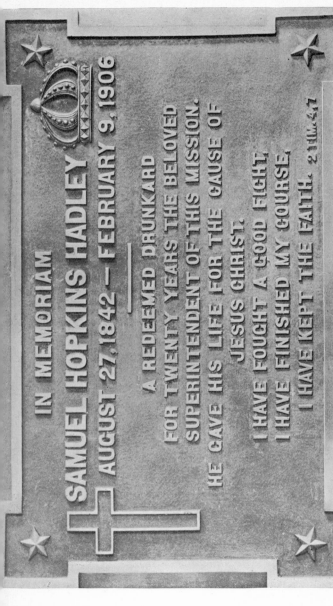

IN MEMORIAM

SAMUEL HOPKINS HADLEY

AUGUST 27, 1842 — FEBRUARY 9, 1906

A REDEEMED DRUNKARD
FOR TWENTY YEARS THE BELOVED
SUPERINTENDENT OF THIS MISSION.
HE GAVE HIS LIFE FOR THE CAUSE OF
JESUS CHRIST.

I HAVE FOUGHT A GOOD FIGHT,
I HAVE FINISHED MY COURSE,
I HAVE KEPT THE FAITH. 2 TIM. 4:7

TABLET OF S. H. HADLEY.

was one of seven that three or four years ago formed what we called our own little circle; and we agreed that every Saturday night as long as we lived at the hour most convenient to us before we retired, we would each ask God's blessing upon the others and upon the particular work in which they might be engaged. That circle is broken so far as this earth is concerned; but in talking with two of the members we each expressed the same idea that we would never ask anyone to take his place in that circle: for we expect every Saturday night that he will be with us in spirit, and therefore we shall go on until there is only one left on earth.

"I wonder, dear friends, if there is a single unsaved soul in this room? I do believe this meeting would not be blessed of God unless an invitation were here given by the side of these dear remains. You know what he would have said if he were here. 'Twenty-three years, nine months and twenty days ago I gave my heart to the Lord Jesus Christ.' We are going to close this meeting with prayer, and I want to ask anybody in this room if they feel as though the Lord Jesus Christ were present here by His Holy Spirit to raise his or her hand, and by so doing say I want an interest in this prayer, and in this meeting.

Rev. Ford C. Ottman, D. D., one of Mr. Hadley's truest friends, closed the service with prayer.

The service at Water Street was closed by the singing of "Oh, it is Wonderful!" by the audience, and of "I must tell Jesus," by the quartet.

XVII

FUNERAL SERVICES AT JOHN STREET METHODIST CHURCH

AFTER the services had been concluded at Water Street a great company of redeemed men followed the hearse bearing the precious remains through the streets of the lower part of New York; following these men came the Trustees, a number of them New York's most representative business men, and following the Trustees came a great company of sorrowing friends, many of whom could not refrain from weeping as they realised the loss they had sustained in the going away of this man of God. Special seats had been reserved at the old John Street church. The building was crowded, the audience being packed out into the streets. The services in the church were opened with prayer, Dr. John Willis Baer being called upon for the invocation. He prayed as follows:

"God, our Father in Heaven, though our eyes be filled with tears yet we do not come to-day to mourn a defeat, but to celebrate a victory; and although we find our tongues faltering, yet our hearts are conscious of the same abiding faith that our friend had in his everyday life. This will be for some of us a strange world without him, and yet we must go on. O God, teach us how to love the way that man loved. Teach us how to refuse to be disappointed in man and never

194

to be discouraged; show us how more and more we can have so much of Thee, that everyone seeing us will see Thee. And as we gather here at this casket side this noon, we turn our eyes with the eyes of faith to the very gates of heaven, and rejoice that with him to-day there are bright stars for his crown. O God, may we never go empty handed before Thee. And we ask Thee that every word that shall be said and done here now shall be of that kind that would not only please him were he with us, as he is, but will help us all in our lives to go on and fight, and fight, and fight harder for Thee. Be with everyone that has been led to Thee by him. Let every man understand now more than he ever understood before that God expects him to do his best and to pick up this work and carry it forward until the last day. Give us a continual and abiding interest in it for the sake of Jesus Christ. Amen."

The pastor, Dr. Johnson, asked the quartet to finish the hymn that had been commenced in Water Street, "I must tell Jesus."

Dr. J. Ross Stevenson, who read the first lesson, said: "No more appropriate Scripture lesson could be found, and no more appropriate commentary on the life of our dear friend could be found than the 13th chapter of 1st Corinthians, which I shall read."

Dr. Randall J. North read 1st Cor. xv. 41-58 as the second Scripture lesson.

Miss Bertha Irene Chapman sang, "Thy Will be Done."

At this point Dr. A. T. Pierson spoke, saying:

"There are two ways of looking at such an event as this. One is to look at it as the close of a life;

the other way is to look at it as the beginning of a life. Looking at it as the close of a life I am impressed that there is not a man living that is adequate to write a true story of the career of S. H. Hadley. I have never known a man that equalled him as a winner of souls. I do not believe that the Church of Jesus Christ in this country has sustained so severe a loss in half a century as it sustains to-day. Hadley was a Christian statesman.

"There are seven problems that confront society that the wisest men in the church and in the state have found themselves unable to solve: the problem of drink; the problem of lust; the problem of crime; the problem of labour and capital; the problem of distance between church and masses; the problem of the uplifting of American negroes; and the problem of reaching the outcast classes. While we have been talking about the last problem Samuel H. Hadley has been working, and while we have been scheming to solve it he has been practically solving it. God has His Hall of Fame, but no human judges determine who shall have a monument and a memorial within it. God sees not as man sees; man looks on the outward appearance, but the Lord looketh upon the heart. But He gives us some conception in His blessed Word as to the conditions of a place within the Celestial Hall of Fame. Those are counted worthy of a place there who have a simplicity like that of a little child, who have a soul humility, and are great in God's eyes because they are little in their own; and especially those who are willing to learn the sweet lesson of cheerful sacrifice of self for the salvation of others. I submit to anyone that knew Mr.

Hadley whether he had not these three great attributes and characteristics: a childlike simplicity, a lowly humility, and a mighty passion for human souls. He has learned that suffering is the price of service. If ever a man learned the lesson of cheerful self-abnegation it was Samuel Hadley. He was content to starve that others might be fed; to deprive himself of what seemed necessary that more imperative needs might be supplied. He would take off his coat to clothe a naked man, and he would give away his last cent to help a poor one. But in nothing was he more remarkable than in the inexhaustible patience that he manifested toward those whom he sought to help.

"I said to him one day, 'Hadley, don't you often get cheated?' He said, 'Cheated is no word for it.' 'Does your patience never give out?' He replied, 'Never, by God's grace. His patience has never given out with me. If a man beats me nineteen times I shame him by trusting him the twentieth.' And this was the simple truth about this wonderfully Christlike man. I tell you, beloved, some of us who have perhaps been more conspicuous before the public eye will take a back seat in the heavenly mansions and see him march to the front line.

"But there is quite another way to look at this event, as the beginning of another life. I think one of the severest tests of the genuineness of our Christianity is a funeral occasion. We give to the world a great deal of flat contradiction of our theories when we come to stand about the bier of the dead. We profess to believe that death is the vestibule to an eternal life; that to pass through death as a Christian believer is to enter into the presence of the Lord

Jesus and the company of glorified saints. But no outsider looking upon many of our gatherings around the body of the dead would have any idea that we held so sublime and so uplifting a doctrine. I have been seeking, especially in the later years of my life, to rise to an attitude where I could make the truth Jesus taught us in Christian faith a reality to myself and those about me, and to act as I stand beside the bier of such a man as Hadley somewhat as I believe our Lord Jesus Christ would have us act in the presence of the death of a saint. We must not forget his infinite gain in our unspeakable loss; we must think of him as in the presence of the Jesus whom he so devotedly loved. ' The lame man leaps as an hart,' and his eyes with transfigured vision look on the glory of the Christ whom he loved, adored, and imitated.

" Now there are four Scriptures that I would like to bring to your notice with great brevity, but simply by way of suggestion. They let a flood of light upon the whole subject of the believer's death.

" The first is what Christ said to the Sadducees. You know they were the doubters of His day; they not only believed that there was no resurrection for the body, but that there was no disembodied existence for the spirit. And Christ said to them by way of rebuke that God was called the God of Abram and of Isaac and of Jacob, and He said, ' God is not the God of the dead, but of the living, for all live unto Him,' and the only way to understand those words is to understand that He represented those whom we call dead as living. This man is not dead; he never lived before in the highest sense. You look upon not Hadley, but

Hadley's discarded mortal tenement. As Socrates said, 'You may bury me if you can catch me.' It is not in the power of anybody to bury S. H. Hadley. The Hadley we love is there [pointing upwards].

"Then I want you to notice what our Lord said about the Father's house of many mansions. And the Father's house isn't merely heaven; the Father's house is the universe. Every house is built by someone, but He that built all things is God. The Father's house is the universe. This is part of it. There are other mansions higher up, beyond the mist and the clouds, and death is the leaving of the lower apartments and going up the golden spiral staircase to the higher rooms. We must not think of death as the cessation of existence, or the interruption of existence. It is the change of sphere. And this beloved man has simply gone out of the low, dark, damp, earth-room; the curtain has fallen behind him, and he has gone up the shining stairs to the upper apartments, to look out beyond clouds and darkness and shadow on the eternal realities of God.

"Now, there is another Scripture I'll call your attention to. I will not tarry longer, but it is the most important of all. In the fourteenth chapter of Revelations occurs that marvellous post-Pentecostal view of death: 'And I heard a voice from heaven saying unto me, Write, Blessed are the dead which die in the Lord from henceforth; Yea, saith the Spirit, that they may rest from their labours; and their works do follow them.'

"Now, I submit to anyone who knows the original that these words do not properly convey the sense of the original. In the first place, will you notice the two words that seem to us synonymous, 'labours' and 'works.' They are not the same in the English; they are not the same in the original. 'They rest from their labours'; that word means 'toils that are vexatious,' toils that imply brain sweat and brow sweat, discouragement and difficulty, toils where we have all we can do to get through with the work. When the Christian dies he rests from all his vexatious and toilsome labour. 'Works' mean 'activities.' Activities don't cease when a man dies; they then more gloriously begin. And although that word is translated 'follow,' the original is 'go with them.' They rest from their toilsome, vexatious labour, but their holy activities go with them into the world beyond. Do you suppose that man is idle? My friends, he has got more to do for God than he ever had.

"Charles Haddon Spurgeon said, 'Do you suppose that when I die I, who have preached to 8,000 people on every Lord's Day, am going to do nothing? I may be preaching to 50,000 where I preach to 5,000.' Some work God has for S. H. Hadley, and his activities have gone with him into the eternal. What his work is we don't know, but you don't suppose that God is going to train a man for service, and then just as he is ready for service take him away from all spheres of service? Do you suppose they sit up there on golden chairs meditating? 'They rest not day nor night,' not only from acts of worship, but from acts of service.

"I feel ashamed when I go through our cemeteries and see the memorials of our dead. I went through a cemetery one day and watched the memorials, broken columns over Christians' graves, quenched fires, flowers plucked from their stems, withered and fallen to pieces, the memorials of defeat, despair, disaster, and destruction. And the only memorial I saw that was fit for a Christian was a full-sculptured sheaf of wheat over the grave of the worst man I ever knew.

"That is the way our Christian faith contradicts our Christian testimony; that is the way our Christian testimony contradicts our Christian faith. My beloved, let me give you as I sit down an epitaph for Samuel Hadley. I would like to see these words engraved upon the headstone where his body lies:

"'When the ear heard me, then it blessed me; and when the eye saw me, it gave witness to me; because I delivered the poor that cried, and the fatherless, and him that had none to help him. The blessing of him that was ready to perish came upon me; and I caused the widow's heart to sing for joy. I was eyes to the blind, and feet was I to the lame. I was a father to the poor.'"

J. Wilbur Chapman delivered the funeral oration, which was as follows:

"Dear friends, I feel we have come to-day to pay our tribute not only to one of the greatest men that New York has produced, but I feel as if I had the right to say that we have come to pay our tribute to one of the greatest men that our country has known in a generation. We never could measure his greatness in money, although I suppose very few men in Christian work have been able to command so great means as he. You never could measure his greatness in fame, as men speak of fame.

"But if you measure his greatness in love for the lost, and in a passion for souls, and in a desire to be like Jesus Christ, he was the greatest man that New York has seen in a century. And I can say with truth to-day that I had rather with this memory be Samuel H. Hadley lying here in this casket, with all these sorrowing friends about, but rejoicing while they sorrow, than to be any other living man I know. If I speak briefly to-day you will attribute it, I am sure, to a full heart, and if I should speak brokenly, I am sure you will attribute it to an expression of the sense of sorrow which I feel this afternoon.

"It is as if one were called to stand beside the casket of his brother, and yet he was more to me than a brother. It is as if one should be asked to stand by the casket of a member of his own household and try to say these words, for I think I loved him as I love one of my own flesh and blood. He was the dearest soul I have ever known, and the greatest. For twenty-three years, nine months, and seventeen days he served the Lord Jesus Christ. He was great any way you may look at him.

"He had a great ancestry. The blood of Jonathan Edwards throbbed in his veins, and I suppose that gave him something of his concern for the lost. His father was a great man; his mother was a sweet, gentle soul. Dr. Pierson said over in Water Street that he never had heard anybody speak the name of Jesus as Samuel Hadley spoke it. There is another name I should like to add to that: I think I never heard anybody say the word 'mother' as he said it. I have sat by his side in the railroad train, visited with him in my home, and never tired of hearing him tell the story of his noble mother. He was a great man in his ancestry.

"In the second place, he had a great fall; he made a sad wreck of his life. I have heard his story, I suppose, hundreds of times, and I never have heard him tell of the depths of his shame that I have not felt myself shudder. I have said every time I have heard him tell his story, 'Surely, that cannot be so!' He was a man of the finest spirit I have ever seen; he hated everything that was mean and low. And to imagine this dear, sweet soul as having ever gone to the depths of sin described by him so often is to me an inconceivable thing. He made a great wreck of his life.

"But he had a great repentance. Not long ago I heard the Bishop of Connecticut preach an evangelistic sermon; he was speaking about repentance, and said that when one repented he had to go back as far to God as he had gone away from Him. But I thought as I sat listening to the Bishop that the difference between coming back and going away was this, that when you went back you had Jesus with you. So this man wandered far away from Him; but in all these twenty-three years, nine months, and seventeen days he kept step with Jesus Christ as I never have known a man to keep step. He was the most like Jesus Christ as he limped his way through the streets of our city and into our homes of any man I have ever seen. And I had rather have my friends say that about me, and so would you, than to have them say that I was the greatest man the world had ever known.

"He had a great recovery from his falling away from God, and the great recovery was manifested in the complete transformation of his nature. I never have known a man that had such a passion for souls. I have heard him say that he used to swear in his sleep. I look down at that precious face to-day, and think of those lips ever framing an oath, and think of them as I have heard him preach the glorious Gospel of the Cross as I never heard any man preach it, and I say, ' What a marvellous transformation! ' That is grace. I never have known a man in all my ministry, as Dr. Pierson has said, that would go as far after the lost, wait so long for them to return, deal with them so patiently, and love them so persistently as this man who had the great recovery in Jesus Christ.

" And he always preached a great salvation. There never was a man too low for him. He used to say at our Bible Conference that when men were kicked out of every other place in the city they had their best welcome at Water Street. I have never read the announcement of his services in the Saturday papers that my eyes haven't been blurred with tears and my heart hasn't given a great bound when he has written, ' Everybody welcome, drunkards especially.' There never was a man so far away but S. H. Hadley had a Gospel for him. There never was a woman so depraved in all this world but he had a word of cheer for; and there are women to-day in this city of New York who feel as if they had lost indeed the best friend that ever lived for them in the going away of this saint of God. He had a great recovery.

" I have been told that at the foot of the cliff over against the Castle Merrion, the castle that used to be occupied by the Emperor Maximilian of Mexico, that away down eighty feet below the surface of the Adriatic there is a little bit of a crevice that has been cut in the cliff, and down in that cleft there are some of the most priceless pearls that are known. They belong to an archduchess. They have not been worn for a long time, and experts decided that the only thing that could bring back their brilliancy was to give them this continual bath in the sea. And these experts say that these pearls which have gone ' sick,' as the experts say, are now coming back to their old brilliancy. And pearl-fishers say that the deeper the water the more priceless the pearl. I do not know whether that is true or not, but I do know this, dear friends, that what the sea is doing to-day for those priceless pearls of the archduchess, Samuel H. Hadley did for lost men here in this city of New York. Mr. Edwards, I wish you would stand up just a moment; you can do it. This is the first man that Samuel Hadley ever won to Jesus Christ after taking charge of the Water Street Mission. Stand out near the casket, Mr. Edwards; you will like to stand near him. And if we had time this afternoon I should ask all of these men to file past this casket, and ask you to sit and look on. Oh, but he preached a marvellous salvation. His was a great, great story, this life transformed and transfigured, and the lives of hundreds of men in and outside of this church. Do you wonder that I say to-day, dear friends, that I consider him one of the greatest men that our city as well as our land has known? Remain standing there a moment, Mr. Edwards, though I know it will cause the tears of some of you to flow as you sit looking into his face, but you will love my brother more.

" The first time I ever saw him was in a dive in this city. I was preaching near this city, and one of my friends said, 'Would you like to see New York at its worst?' I said, 'I would.' He said, 'Come with me, and I'll give you a guide.' We came across the ferry and went down to the lowest part of the city, and there I saw this man of God. He said, 'I'll take you into some of the saloons.' I saw him throw his arms about a poor, drunken man and cry over him. I walked with him into a place of ill-fame, and I saw him lay his hand on the head of a young girl painted and sinful, and saw the hot tears rain down his cheeks and fall upon her upturned face. I saw him go into one of the lowest dens of the city and take in his arms just as many people as could get near him, and I heard him sing. It was the sweetest singing I have ever heard. I have heard Patti sing, but Patti never thrilled me as this man thrilled me whenever he sang. And when we came out of this place of sin he stopped for a moment under the gaslight, and I looked up into his face, and he said, 'Well, I must be going now. Good-night.' He limped away a few steps and then he came back and took my hand, and gave it one of those pressures that were so peculiar to him, and he said, 'Oh, oh, oh, oh!' Haven't you heard him say it? 'Oh, oh, oh, oh! brother, as long as you live,' he said, 'preach a Christ that can save these lost people.' And if there has been any tenderness in my preaching, if there has been any special passion for lost men and women, I owe it in part to the saint of God who lies here so still in our presence to-day.

"The last time I saw him was a short time ago. I was sitting alone in a room, when I heard that peculiar thump, thump, thump of his cane in the hallway; the door opened, and in he walked, the sweetest smile on his face I have almost ever seen; and he said, 'I thought I'd just come and visit with you. I am a little bit tired, and I thought I'd just like to come and visit with you.' While in the city he told his matchless story, made his last appeal to men; and as I went to a midnight meeting in the theatre, he threw his arm around my shoulder, the last time for this world, and he said, 'Good-bye; when we go south together I'll give you three weeks of my time, and we'll see what we can do in Texas to win the drunkards for Christ. Good-bye.' And he went away, to stay until I see him with you in the resurrection morning.

"Between those two experiences with him there has stretched out the most beautiful life I have ever known.

"Add one more picture and you have his beautiful life complete. Mrs. Hadley tells me that while this precious body was lying in the Mission last night there came up a man who once before had claimed to follow Christ, but had drifted away from Him, and he threw his arms round about the casket, and bent over with the hot tears raining down his cheeks, and said, 'Samuel Hadley, when he was alive, gave me one vision of Christ, and now that he is dead I want to have another.' That was his life. Oh, you matchless man of God, I never have known your like, never.

"I want to close with just a word by saying he was a true friend. Did any of you ever have a better friend? Jim Edwards, did you ever have a better friend? No, and no other man ever did.

"He left me two precious treasures. When he was

sending his greetings to his friends, as he did to many of you, my brethren, he spoke my name with those lips of his, and said, 'Just tell Chapman that I can do him more good at the Throne than I could do him here.' I rather imagine I shall have a better ministry from to-day. I rather believe that I shall preach a sweeter story from to-day.

"The other inheritance is this [holding aloft Mr. Hadley's familiar cane]. He doesn't need it. As Dr. Pierson says, 'The lame shall leap as an hart.' He doesn't need it.

"He was a great example of love. He was a cultured Christian gentleman. He had that rare talent and ability of going down to lost men, poor, depraved drunkards, and outcast women, making them feel that he was one of them; and yet he had the ability of going into the homes of wealth in New York, and he never crossed a threshold but the richest people in the land didn't feel they had met their equal. He was a true gentleman, a true gentleman. He was a great man.

"We had at our Bible Conference, where he came every year for ten blessed, happy years, some of the greatest men that this country has ever known. We had that matchless intellectual giant, Dr. Francis Patten. I remember one evening, when Dr. Patten had just lifted us up to the throne of grace, and we had almost gone through the gates, Mr. Hadley came up to him and said, 'Doctor, some of those big words of yours just about flabbergasted me, they just about did.' But the tears rolled down his cheeks as he said, 'But you know I love Jesus better since I heard you speak than I ever loved Him before.' Dr. Patten

CHARLES YATES.

HARRY E. PRENTICE.

looked back at him and said, 'Mr. Hadley, nobody moves me like you, nobody.' The ministers all loved him.

" Mr. Bowne was right when he said the world seems lonesome without him. I don't know how in the world we'll ever get on. New York seems to me as if a great part of it had moved out. It must seem so to you, my brethren; really the best part of it for me has gone. We have a sense of loneliness to-day such as we have not known in years. Some of us will never be the same again, never. Some of our family circles will never be the same again. Mine never will. One of my children has prayed for Mr. Hadley since she first learned to talk, 'God bless Mr. Hadley and the Water Street Mission.'

" It was always a great gala day in our home when S. H. Hadley arrived; from the smallest baby in the household to myself we lined up to see him come in; and we all of us said, ' Now, so long as he's here we'll not any of us work. We'll just sit around and love him.' And we laughed and cried and all but shouted from the moment he came in until he went out. We have a broken family circle in our household, and I suppose the most of you have.

" There must have been a great commotion in heaven when he went in. Yesterday must have been a high day in heaven. The first Sunday in Glory! Can you imagine it?

" I have a friend, the Rev. Henry Ostrom, D. D., who tells the following story of the visit of William Arthur to this country, and of his telling the students in one of the seminaries about an old friend of his, Robert Sutcliffe, who was very dangerously ill, and an old friend of the two of them, Dr. Mahan, went to see him. He took the old man's hand, and he said, ' Robert, did you know that Benson had gone home? ' The old saint said, ' Benson gone home? ' ' Yes, and did you know that so-and-so had gone? ' giving the name of a mutual friend. ' What, has he gone? ' ' Yes, and did you know that so-and-so had gone? ' naming still another. ' No, has he gone, too? ' ' Yes, Robert, everybody seems to have gone but you and me of the old circle.' Robert Sutcliffe lay still for a moment; then he opened his eyes and smiled, and said, ' I rather think that some of those old friends up in glory have met together and they have been looking around for me, and they must have said, " Where's Robert Sutcliffe? He must have lost his way." ' Then his eyes were shut for a moment, but presently he opened them, and the sweetest smile came across his features as he said, ' I'll soon be there, and I can hear Benson and all the rest of them shouting down the streets of Glory, " Here comes Robert Sutcliffe! He hasn't lost his way! " '

" I think it was like that with our beloved friend. I can well believe Jerry McAuley must have met him; I think his own dear brother surely greeted him; I believe the Old Colonel must have saluted him; I am sure ' Phil ' McGuire must have thrown his arms around him; I imagine that all the redeemed drunkards in heaven must have filled the arches of the Glory shouting, ' Here comes S. H. Hadley! Here he comes! He hasn't lost his way.'

" Farewell, dear friend, farewell. One of these days we shall meet, all of us, in glory. And until that day God give us the passion for souls that you possessed, and until that day God give us the Spirit of Jesus with which you were filled. Farewell."

The quartet sang " The King's Business."

The Rev. Dr. Frank Mason North offered the closing prayer, and the last hymn sung was " Just As I Am."

XVIII

NOTABLE MEMORIAL SERVICES

NUMEROUS services were held in memory of the Superintendent of the Water Street Mission. Rich and poor alike seemed to delight to do him honour.

No more notable service was held, however, than that in the Fifth Avenue Presbyterian Church, one of the greatest churches not only in the Presbyterian denomination, but in the United States. The church is located at Fifth Avenue and Fifty-fifth Street in the heart of the most aristocratic section of New York City. It has been a church of notable gatherings, but none more notable than this; and a church of great pastors.

The Rev. John Hall, D. D., served this church for years, and when he died great men seemed to vie with each other to say great things about him, but nothing better was said about the notable preacher than about the humble servant of Jesus Christ, the Superintendent of the Water Street Mission.

The Rev. George T. Purves, D. D., succeeded Dr. Hall, and after a brief ministry passed to his reward, but the work of so distinguished a preacher as Dr. Purves was not more notable than that of S. H. Hadley.

The Rev. J. Ross Stevenson, D. D., is the present pastor, but Dr. Stevenson himself confessed that to have had S. H. Hadley in his church was one of the greatest privileges in his ministry, and to have the memorial service held in the Fifth Avenue Church was an honour not to be lightly esteemed.

The following is the order of service printed and distributed Sunday afternoon, February 25, 1906:

FIFTH AVENUE PRESBYTERIAN CHURCH.
FIFTH AVENUE AND FIFTY-FIFTH STREET

Minister, Rev. J. Ross Stevenson, D.D., 19 East 66th Street. Telephone, 150 Plaza.

Assistant Minister, Rev. George H. Trull, 600 West 114th Street. Telephone, 5444 Morningside.

ORDER OF AFTERNOON SERVICE.
Four o'clock.

In memoriam Rev. S. H. Hadley, late Supt. of the Water Street McAuley Mission and of Wesley Rescue Hall.

Organ Prelude—Allegretto from 7th Symphony. *Beethoven.*
Anthem—"What are These" . . . . *Stainer.*
Hymn 948.
Introductory Remarks—By Dr. Stevenson.
Address—By Mr. Walter M. Smith, Chairman.
Scripture Lesson and Prayer—By the Rev. Frank Mason North, D.D.
Hymn—Glory Song.
Addresses—By Lieutenant-Governor M. Linn Bruce.
The Rev. J. Wesley Johnston, D.D.
The Rev. Donald Sage Mackay, D.D.
Singing—Messrs. Fitzgerald and Brown.
Testimonies from Converts of the Mission.
Address—By Mr. John Willis Baer.
Hymn 609.
The congregation will resume their seats for the Benediction and for a moment of silent prayer.
Benediction.
Organ Postlude—March from Saul . . . *Handel,*

It was one of the most miserable rainy days of the winter, but that did not prevent some 2,000 people from gathering in this edifice to pay honour to their friend and helper. For two hours the late friend of the outcast was eulogised, and it is very probable that if the weather had been fair, there would not have been standing room in the great church. It was rather an odd audience. Millionaires and their handsomely dressed wives sat alongside of the men of the street and the women of the humblest walks in life. The men from the Mission and also those from the Rescue Home marched to the church in a body and occupied specially reserved seats in the middle aisle near the pulpit; and sprinkled throughout the entire audience were plain people. But some way or other all class distinction seemed to be forgotten in the common purpose of doing honour to Mr. Hadley. Even the regular Presbyterian church hymnals were laid aside, and instead, some of Mr. Hadley's favourite gospel songs were sung with great fervour. The quartet sang "And I Shall See Him Face to Face" and "The Glory Song," and the vast congregation joined in the chorus. There was no note of desolation in the rendering, but rather one of victory.

The Rev. Dr. J. Ross Stevenson, the pastor of the Fifth Avenue Presbyterian Church, made the introductory remarks, and compared Mr. Hadley to St. Paul the Apostle. " If Paul should come to New York, I am afraid he would pass by many of our churches, but his chief interest would be in a work like the McAuley Mission," he said. " Mr. Hadley has immortalised the Water Street Mission. How strong were the rays of mercy and of hope that he sent forth from that lighthouse of God. His influence was not confined to the Mission. It was known at home and abroad. It has been a demonstration to the city that love is the greatest power in the world. Mr. Hadley was also greatly interested in summer religious conferences and in evangelistic enterprises. The city of New York owes him a debt it cannot pay. The work he did was the work we ought to do. This church, like many others, helped support his work. It was our privilege to have him speak here. I want to say that I count it one of the greatest privileges of my life to have known him and to have entertained him in my home. Mr. John S. Huyler, one of the trustees, was to have been here. In the absence of Mr. Huyler, I will place this meeting in charge of Mr. Walter M. Smith, also a trustee."

After Mr. Smith was introduced, he said among other things: " I regret with Doctor Stevenson the absence of Mr. John S. Huyler, for many years president of the McAuley Mission, who was expected to preside at this meeting; he is unavoidably absent. It devolves upon me in behalf of the family of Mr. Hadley, and of the trustees of the Mission, to thank Doctor Stevenson for his kind words, and the officers of this church for the privilege so courteously extended, of holding here this memorial service to one who for twenty years gave 'the best that was in him,' yes, his life, to help the wretched and the lost.

" Samuel H. Hadley endeared himself to every soul with whom he came in contact. He was always welcome in the home of luxury; the thief of the slums met him as a friend; they all knew him; they all loved

him and he loved them.   If ever a man walked in the
footsteps of his Saviour, he was that man.

"We meet here to honour his memory, and in doing
this we honour ourselves."

The Rev. Dr. F. Mason North offered prayer.

"We thank Thee, O God, for giving this man the
willingness to go where Thou didst want him to go,"
said Dr. North in his prayer.   "We thank Thee for
this mediator between the kindness of God and the
misery of men.   May the influence of his life be last-
ing in our city.   We cannot tell where Thou hast
another to do the work he has done.   Our hearts long
for that deeper life and simpler faith which was his."

Lieutenant-Governor Bruce spoke in part as follows:

"As a citizen of this great city and of this State,
I am glad of this opportunity to pay a tribue of respect
to Samuel Hopkins Hadley.   I know that I have but
an inadequate appreciation of his wonderful work
and his heroic service.   Only the shipwrecked mariner,
rescued after all hope has fled, fully appreciates the
self-sacrifice and daring of the life-saver, who, making
his way through surf and storm, brings hope and life.
And it is only the outcasts around whom this great
man placed his strong arms, lifting them out of the
gutters and setting their feet upon the rock, that
feel and know of his mighty works of faith and his
labours of love.

"Samuel H. Hadley needs no memorial, no monument.   Everywhere throughout this broad land there
are thousands of men whose honourable lives testify
to his greatness and his goodness.   They will hold his
memory as the dearest treasure of earth and will hand

it down from generation to generation long after many so-called great men of his time are forgotten.

"But I wish as a citizen to express the debt of gratitude which I feel the city and the State owe Mr. Hadley for his great service in reclaiming from careers of vice and crime thousands of men and women residents of this city, and restoring them to law-abiding, useful citizenship. For twenty-two long years, amid the heat of summer and the cold of winter, he stood at his post in the old Jerry McAuley Mission, under the shadow of the Brooklyn Bridge, rescuing the perishing, caring for the dying, speaking words of hope to the fallen, feeding the hungry, clothing the naked and pleading with the wanderers to return to the Father's house, to begin a life of honour and of self-respect. No matter how often a weak one fell, he never chided, never a word of reproach, never condemned; his pleadings were always words of love, of encouragement and of hope. It is estimated that more than 75,000 men came under Mr. Hadley's personal ministry, thousands of whom are to-day useful members of society.

"The keynote of his life was, 'Not to be ministered unto, but to minister.'"

The Rev. J. Wesley Johnston, D. D., Mr. Hadley's pastor, spoke as follows:

"He was more my pastor than I his pastor. It is only those who have known what it is to have had such a man in the congregation who can sympathise with us," he continued. "Many philanthropists have had severe things to say about the attitude of the church to the poor. I sometimes feel that these reformers are responsible for much of the so-called class distinction. But this was not so with Brother Hadley. He brought all of his manhood to the church and took much from the church in return. These missions, to him, were simply doorways to the church. No man in the last fifty years, not even the great evangelist Moody, has done more to bring the church and the common people together than S. H. Hadley. I declare to you that there is not a church in the United States that is not indebted to this man for what he did in bridging the gap. Hadley never considered any man's reclamation complete until the convert had identified himself with some church. There was nothing superficial about his conversions. Because a man came to the mourner's bench and said he wanted to begin over again Hadley did not consider that all sufficient. With Brother Hadley there was a living figure, a tremendous personality. And he was not content until his converts had been brought face to face with Christ as a living Saviour. And he never recommended a single convert for membership in the church of which I am pastor until he had some guarantee that the man had had such an experience. He laboured to make Christ a real man to every man, and a real Saviour to every sinner. He taught them that it was not a reformation, not a vow or a promise, but that it was only through trust in Christ that they could be reclaimed. God, Heaven, Christ, Redemption—these to him were fibres that entered into his very being. But I affirm he has rendered a service to the church, a service we can never pay. He has rewritten the Acts of the Apostles, and he has written in flesh and blood. He has transferred that which happened two millenniums ago in another land down to to-day over in Water Street, New York. And there he has illustrated again and again the marvellous display of God's power, which was shown in the early church. When Saul stood up before Agrippa and told the story of his conversion, he did not tell it with any more reality than Hadley told of his marvellous regeneration. The question is now, Is the work to stop because he has gone? There are multitudes more, not in the valley of decision, but in the valley of poverty and sin and despair, who are victims of habit and the slaves of appetite. Who will save them? God grant that a man may be raised up."

The next speaker was the Rev. Dr. Donald Sage Mackay, who said in part: " There were three great realities in Mr. Hadley's life—the reality of sin, the reality of conversion, and the reality of service. The man lived a life of apostolic devotion such as is rarely known. In these days when there are so many artificial people, and when so many are flitting their lives away on non-essentials, it is comforting to think of a man spending his time and energy as Hadley did. To him God was a great reality. He lived in the presence of God. It was this that gave him power. He knows of his great results, but we don't know of the hard nights, the bitter experiences, and of the wrestling with God in prayer. This man fought his way day by day. Hadley was not a man of sentiment, but he was a man of profound emotion. He could read character. He could find out whether a man was in earnest. His own conversion was a great reality. He never told it as a matter of history, but always with new life. Scientists are discussing the subject of conversion. Well, friends, hard names

won't do any harm.   But with Hadley, conversion was
the incoming of the Holy Spirit.   With him conversion meant service, and it should be so with everyone.   No conversion was allowed to lax into for-
getfulness.   That life has wrought itself into the
spiritual history of New York, America, the world."

A portion of the exercises was the reading of a
telegram from Rev. Dr. J. Wilbur Chapman, a close
friend and warm admirer of the mission worker, and
who was one of the speakers at his funeral.

" I want to pay a tribute to one of the princes of
men, and to pledge myself in some way to help carry
on his work," wrote Dr. Chapman.   The despatch
was sent from Florida, where Dr. Chapman was attending the Florida Winter Bible Conference.   Another despatch was read from Charles M. Alexander,
the great evangelistic singer, who said he regretted not
being able to attend the memorial service.   From
Dr. Reuben A. Torrey, the evangelist, came the following letter, which eulogised Mr. Hadley.   Both of
the latter messages were sent from Philadelphia,
where Dr. Torrey and Mr. Alexander are holding a
mission.

The following is Dr. Torrey's letter:

" 505 So. 42ND STREET, PHILADELPHIA, PA.,
" *February* 21, 1906.

" I have known Brother Hadley for many years, and
I have loved him as I have loved few men.   He has
taught me to love others as I did not love them before.
One of the greatest blessings of my life came through
a talk that Brother Hadley once gave in my own
church on Love.   I think I have loved the fallen since

that, and have learned to be patient with all men as I never was before. Not only his words, but his life, was a benediction to me. I have had the deepest interest in his work in New York for years. I have rarely visited New York but what I have taken occasion to run over to Water Street Mission at least once. While one is not impressed with the largeness of the meeting at Water Street Mission, the thing that has impressed me has been the solidity of the work. I know many men, personally, who are leading earnest Christian lives to-day, who were once the very off-scouring of the world. I have many a friend who found Christ at the Water Street Mission. We have had a number at the Bible Institute who have come there to study after having been converted at the Mission, and they were men that we loved and honoured.

"I got a great blessing to my own soul from the book 'Down in Water Street,' and it has been a joy to recommend it to others, who have also been blessed and encouraged through reading it. I think that the Water Street Mission under our Brother Hadley has been one of the greatest of present-day illustrations that 'the Gospel is the power of God unto salvation to everyone that believeth.'

"R. A. TORREY."

But the most pronounced feature of the entire programme was the testimonies given by some of the converts of the Water Street Mission and of the home.

"Samuel Hopkins Hadley led me to Jesus. I loved him, and I will follow him to eternity," said a manly-looking fellow. "I was a drunkard. I had Christian parents. When I was a boy I went to Sunday School and church. I took to drinking whiskey. This got me to gambling. Gambling led me to steal. Eight years, one month, and two days ago I wandered into the Water Street Mission. I had slept off two drunks that day, and I went to sleep in the Mission, and Brother Hadley woke me up. And he helped me find Jesus that night."

The assistant superintendent of the Mission said that seventeen years and five months ago he was converted under Mr. Hadley.

" Nineteen years, nine months, and twenty-three days ago," said a great, tall man, " I staggered into the door of that Mission, and I heard S. H. Hadley tell what Jesus had done for him. I have learned this lesson, that no matter how far down a man is, God can pick him up."

There were several others who spoke along the same line. All of these men showed by their appearance that their conversion had been genuine. Just before the closing hymn, which was " Just As I Am Without One Plea," all those present who were converted under Mr. Hadley were asked to rise. Fully 400 men immediately stood up, and for several moments there was a sacred stillness. They responded like soldiers to a call, and they were proud to testify their leader.

Dr. John Willis Baer, formerly Secretary of the Board of Home Missions of the Presbyterian Church, and now President of Occidental College, was the last speaker. " Have you ever thought how Hadley hated?" he asked. " He hated sin, and he hated saloons. If the church of to-day hated the saloon the way Hadley did, it would be swept out of existence.

And have you ever thought how Hadley loved? He loved men back to Christ. O God, that we could love the way Hadley did. His mantle is big enough to fall on all of us. God will possibly never make another Hadley. I believe that to-day Hadley sees you just as you are, not as you appear to be. Oh, how ashamed to-day I am that I did not do more for him. There is a great responsibility resting on every one of us. God has blessed us with certain gifts, and we should consecrate them to His service, as Hadley did. Are we going out of that door any better than we came in? This is our responsibility."

The newspapers of the city of New York, without exception, gave an unusual amount of space to the telling of the story of his life. The New York *World,* under date of February 26, with striking headlines referred to the memorial service as follows:

"RICH, POOR, GOOD, BAD WEPT FOR HADLEY.

" Wealthy Congregation and ' Sinners' Club ' Cry Together at Service for ' Angel.' Memorial Services for the late Samuel Hopkins Hadley, Who Died Feb. 9, After Serving Nineteen Years as the Head of the Old Jerry McAuley Mission in Water Street, Were Held at the Fifth Avenue Presbyterian Church Yesterday Afternoon.

" No greater tribute to the memory of this friend of sinners could be found than was presented by the audience gathered in the fashionable church to listen to the eulogies of the dead man. In the galleries were the silk-clothed congregation of the church, for the most part wealthy persons who knew little of the life of the mission worker. In the body of the great church was gathered a strange assembly of men, women, and children. All of them cried during the service. All of them wore little badges to tell the curious that they were members of the 'Sinners' Club.' The 'Sinners' Club' had been given the place of honour in the rich church.

"As many of the 'club' as could crowd into the seats were there. Many stood in the entry. Some were reformed. Many of them were not. Many bore hard faces left by lives of vice and sorrow. They all knew Samuel Hopkins Hadley personally, and they knew what he had done for their kind. Whether or not they had lived better themselves through his teachings, they were there to testify to the memory of the man who had saved so many of their friends. Reformed thieves, drunkards, social outcasts sat together weeping.

"Lieutenant-Governor M. Linn Bruce was one of the speakers. He had known the mission-worker in life, and he had been by his side in death.

"' "What will become of my poor men?" were the last words of the good man,' said Mr. Bruce. At that the ground floor cried afresh, and when the speaker sat down several shabby-looking men and women arose to pay their tributes. Their tributes were such as were heard in the Water Street Mission every night.

"The fashionable congregation for the most part had never heard these simple, impassioned 'testimonials' before, and it was their turn to cry. The Rev. Dr. J.

Wesley Johnston and the Rev. Dr. Donald Sage Mackay spoke of the life of the mission worker. Samuel Hopkins Hadley was rescued from a life of drunkenness himself in the early 80's, and the speakers dwelt long on his redemption and the thousands he had redeemed. They said that 5,000 persons had been made to lead better lives through the work of this mission 'angel.'

"At the close of the meeting the fashionables from the galleries mingled with the shabby people below, and it was an hour after the services ended that the last little group gathered around members of the 'Sinners' Club' and went away."

The New York preachers' meeting was the fourth religious body to observe a memorial to Samuel Hopkins Hadley. "Old Water Street," "Old John Street," and the venerable Fifth Avenue Presbyterian Church had held solemn services of holy triumph over the memory of their fallen hero, brother and saint. So it was in no sense strange that the gathering of preachers was swelled by the best of the throng who had assembled also at these other shrines.

The memory of S. H. Hadley levels the rich and poor, the high and the low, the fortunate and the less fortunate. And on that sad and tender occasion all voices joined in paying affectionate tribute to "one of the greatest sons of our Christian century."

The services, which were conducted by the officers of the New York City Church Extension and Missionary Society, were characterised by outbursts of ecstatic song, words of mellow sweetness, and tears of godly joy mingled with tears of sorrow that such a conquerer had gone to his native heaven. And after a series of well-chosen eulogies had been spoken, the meeting passed a series of memorial resolutions which pledged all to fill up the gap and make up the hedge where Brother Hadley had fallen.

" A sad duty devolves upon us at this time in recording the death of one of our Board of Managers, the Rev. S. H. Hadley, for many years the superintendent of the far-famed Jerry McAuley Mission in Water Street, and the superintendent of the Rescue Mission on the Bowery.

" Few men in Methodism were more widely known than Brother Hadley, and few have left behind them a more enviable record as a successful evangelist and a winner of souls for Christ.

" Having experienced when in the depths of sin a conversion as definite as that of Saul of Tarsus, he was able to preach with a singular power the blessed Gospel of the grace of God, and point lost men and women to One who could save to the uttermost. For more than twenty years it was his supreme joy to tell the story of redeeming love, and this he did with such tenderness, such pathos, such simple unaffected eloquence, and with such manifest approval of God, that thousands were translated from the power of darkness into the kingdom of God's dear Son.

" To the poor, the outcast, the sinful, the abandoned, he was as a chosen apostle, labouring among them with a love that was divine, a tenderness that was Christlike, a sympathy that was inexhaustible, and a patience only possible to such a nature as his.

" He was a man of rare quality, a combination of exquisite degree, having the power to win earnest attention from both high and low, rich and poor, and never failing everywhere to impress himself as a disciple of the Lord Jesus. We earnestly pray that the great work to which he so faithfully devoted his ministry may go on with unabated energy and success.

"To Mrs. Hadley, who has been so devoted to the same glorious work as her now sainted husband, and to his associates and helpers in the Rescue Missions, we extend our sincere sympathies, and pray that God's richest blessings may rest upon their labours."

XIX

HIS MONUMENT

S H. HADLEY has left many an enduring monument of his work. He was the immediate successor of Jerry McAuley, and built well upon the foundation laid by that most distinguished of all rescue mission workers in his day. He was also in a sense the founder of the Wesley Rescue Hall, the name of which has since been changed to the Hadley Hall. He made the following address when the founding of this second mission was under consideration:

"I have the honour, the pleasure, to be in the old Jerry McAuley Mission. We seek men that are lost because they are lost; for no other reason but because nobody loves them. I was once speaking in the penitentiary, and I asked the men to come and see me when their time was up, and, oh, how many of them came. I have been ordained a Methodist preacher. They had to jump over the discipline pretty strongly to accomplish it, but they did it. I preached in the prison once, and I invited eight hundred men to come to see me. I have said: 'If you are sober men, I'm glad to see you, and if you are drunk, I'm glad to see you, too. Come without spending your money.' I say to them: 'There's a man who wants to see you down in Water Street.' I never give that invitation but it has cost me a thousand dollars. There's hardly a meeting given in our Mission but that some men from there who've been invited have come to our place and been saved, and are standing up testifying to the salvation of God. And they received that invitation in the penitentiary.

" Now the Methodist Church has not a Rescue Mission in its whole boundaries. The only two mission reports given here to-day were in Allegheny and Pittsburgh. Some of you have talked about raising debts. When you were boys, your dear old fathers were preachers, and they thought of only one thing —to get men on their knees before God and shouting happy, and then there was not much trouble about raising money or raising the devil, or anything else. Now we have forgotten that. In our city, New York, we ought to have on the Bowery—on the great thoroughfare to hell—we ought to have a Rescue Mission —not a woodyard, or a mothers' meeting, or a kindergarten, but a Rescue Mission, a great, beautiful place to hold four or five hundred, a cheery place lighted up, with a banner outside telling what is inside, that you could see a mile, and inside a lot of saved men who can sing and pray and terrify the devil. We ought to get in the great public, the great unreached masses. My very soul aches for it—the poor, helpless, dying, drunken men! Nobody cared for me. I didn't know a Christian in New York, not one. And I had been here a long time. That's what we ought to do. Every Methodist minister would be electrified by it. Some would perhaps go forward for prayers. They would get really converted.

" The Methodist Church ought to do this work. I was raised in a log Methodist church. My father built it on our farm. Jacob Young preached in it once.

There was one hymn-book and one Bible in the house. Our benches were of the thickness of rails. Sometimes the rails would warp and one leg stick up in the air, but they were benches, 'mourners' benches.' I have seen wonders of God's saving grace. I have seen men fall and lie as posts for hours, and not one but came to and was a faithful Christian to his death.

"New York City ought to have a rescue mission. The Presbyterians have Rescue Missions; the Baptists have Rescue Missions; the Episcopalians have, but we haven't. In the lower part of our city the percentage of Christians is hardly worthy of our mention. It is greater in Calcutta and Bombay, in portions of China, than in New York City below Fourteenth Street. We can't get rid of it until the judgment day, and we say we are not able. We could do much more than we do. We start a church in the suburbs and the members pack their traps and leave the lower part of the city to the devil."

Wesley Hall, now known as Hadley Hall, was opened for work and worship on Saturday evening, March 12, 1904.

Fully 450 people found their way to this unaccustomed place on Saturday night. Over the door in large letters of light they saw "Wesley Rescue Hall." Passing through the long hallway, brilliantly lighted with electricity, they came to the ample assembly room—a great, rough loft transformed by tool and brush and light into one of the brightest and most attractive mission halls in our city.

The services were simple, informal, reverent. While the people gathered some hymns were heartily sung. The corresponding secretary of the society called upon

Dr. E. S. Osborn, Mr. J. F. Cryer, and Dr. G. E. Strobridge to offer prayer. He then, after a short statement, introduced Dr. J. W. Johnston, of John Street Church, and Dr. C. S. Wing, presiding elder of the district in which the mission is located, to speak for the Committee. Then Dr. Louis Klopsch, also a member of the board and president of the Bowery Mission, most felicitously welcomed the new work. Bishop Andrews followed with earnest and appropriate words, and, inviting the people to stand and join in a prayer of consecration, solemnly dedicated this new hall to the unique and blessed work for which it has been prepared.

But the most enduring monument left by Mr. Hadley will be the lives of those whom he had the privilege of leading to Jesus Christ. It is impossible to mention all the names which should be recorded in this book in connection with such a chapter. There is Benjamin Watson, who was a drunken tramp and converted over seventeen years ago; Joseph G. Hester, an Englishman, who was found by Mr. Hadley as he was almost freezing to death and taken into the Mission and saved. There is C. C. Fowler, who occupied a position of trust in one of the great New York houses and was slain by the power of strong drink, only to be rescued by the grace of God; Harry E. Prentice, also an Englishman, brought to the Mission by a companion and started the first night for Christ, and for five years Mr. Hadley's assistant; Arthur H. Rice, who for fifteen years has been kept by the power of God, after he had travelled around the world for assistance and failed to find it; Peter E. Youngblood, whose parents were foreign missionaries, stationed at

Borneo, sent to this country to be educated, graduated at Rutgers, but slain by his appetite, and afterwards rescued by the power of God; Frank F. Fitzgerald, one of the sweetest singers in the country, who was an opera singer and member of a famous quartet, but finally was reduced by sin to singing in the gin mills of New York,—he, too, was saved. He with others sang at Mr. Hadley's funeral, and while in Canton, Ohio, about one year ago was asked to sing for the wife of the martyred President, McKinley. W. L. Anderson, who says that words cannot describe his past sinful life, was converted in 1898, and writes: "Now I have a home of my own, a dear wife and baby, for all of which I thank God." E. C. Mercer, also saved by the grace of God, and now associated with Mr. Wyburn in the Water Street Mission. All these and hundreds of others should be mentioned at length, but material concerning them has not been sent me, and so I can only say, that in almost every city in the land, and possibly in almost every city in the world, there is to be seen to-day some fruit of the work of this distinguished servant of Jesus Christ.

HIS FIRST CONVERT

Mr. Hadley's first convert was James C. Edwards. The following is his testimony:

"1621 67th St., BROOKLYN.

"Rev J. WILBUR CHAPMAN,
       "Winona Lake, Ind.

"MY DEAR SIR AND BROTHER:
   "Some few weeks ago you sent me a letter in regard to our late brother, S. H. Hadley. I may state

that the first time I saw him was about twenty-two years ago, but I never became acquainted with him until the night of the 30th of May, 1886, and since that time I have been very close to him until the day he went home to glory.

" You ask me to say something about him. Well, all I can say is that I as well as thousands of others have missed not only a friend, but a brother, for if there ever was a Christian man it was S. H. Hadley. He was a man the image of our Saviour. When I had troubles or trials I would go to him at 316 Water Street and talk and tell him about it. We would pray, and the warm shake of his hand, and ' God bless you, Jim,' I will never forget. Of course you know how much I loved him.

" I would have answered your letter sooner, but I waited until I celebrated the twentieth anniversary of a Christian life. Now, Brother Chapman, in regard to my conversion, you can get it in the book of S. H. Hadley, ' Down in Water Street.'

> " With prayers, I remain,
>> " Yours in His Name,
>>> " JAMES C. EDWARDS.

" ' Scottie the Bum,' 1886.
" J. C. EDWARDS, 1906."

TOM FARMER'S TESTIMONY

" Two years ago to-night I wandered into this Mission, and knelt down at this front bench and cried to God to be merciful to me, a poor sinner, and I know my prayer was heard and answered, and that God sealed me for His own that night.

"I was born and raised in this city. My father owned and ran a saloon on Washington Street for thirty-five years. I began to steal before I was ten years old. I may not tell this story in detail again, but I want to tell it to-night, so that you may see what God has brought me out of. It is not a pleasant story for me to relate, but I want to do it in order to show you how, if a man will trust Jesus, He will bring him out of darkness into light.

"I started first to tap tills in this city. From that I used to snatch pocketbooks from people in the vicinity of the Desbrosses Street Ferry. My own people knew what I was, and it cost them hundreds of dollars to keep me out of trouble. When my father died he left me several thousand dollars. After getting the money I started for the West. I went from here to Philadelphia. In the State of Pennsylvania I started out on a criminal career that cost me many years in prison. I robbed a post office in that State, was arrested, but was acquitted, but it cost me $800 to get out of that scrape. I then went to California, and was not there long before I was arrested on a charge of highway robbery, and was convicted and sentenced to San Quentin Prison. After serving my sentence there, I had to leave the State at once, as there were enough charges against me to send me up for life. I then went to the State of Oregon, and continued in the highway business, but had to get out of that State pretty quick. Next I drifted into Montana. I was arrested in that State for burglary, and got five years in Deer Lodge Penitentiary. Upon my release from that prison I went to the State of Washington and in the city of Tacoma was arrested on several charges of burglary and highway robbery, but escaped from jail and turned all hands loose with me. I then went back to Seattle and was arrested again on two charges of highway robbery, but managed to get away. I went back to try and get my partners away from the officers, but was caught. While in jail await-ing trial, we nearly managed to escape again by tun-nelling our way out, and would have succeeded but for a United States prisoner, who squealed on us, and I was sent to Walla Walla Prison for seven years.

" While in Walla Walla I plotted to escape. I gave a man money to bring me in a couple of guns. While in this prison they made us work in a brick yard, and while we had it all arranged to grab the warden and throw him on the engine that came in the yard, and in that way escape, as one of my pals said he knew how to run the engine; when we got on the engine, however, instead of running out of the yard, he ran the engine further into the prison yard, and both my pals were shot dead by my side. They caught me and gave me eighteen months in solitary confinement, and for the first twenty days they hardly gave me any water to drink, or any bread to eat. After being released from this prison I was nearly dead, and they took me down to the train, and sent me out of the State into Oregon, but I came back to the State of Washington in a few weeks. It was while in this State that my partners and myself planned to hold up a train. I stationed my partners at the entrance to the cars, while I went through and took all the money and valuables; while I was in the car, however, my partners got cold feet, and deserted me, and matters got so hot for me that I had to drop the bag and run. Bullets were flying all around me, but I managed to escape without injury.

" A short while afterward my partners blew open a safe in a little town just outside of Spokane Falls, and two weeks later myself and my pals were arrested, and the goods found on me; my pals turned State's evidence and got two years in prison. I stood trial and beat the case and was acquitted.

" I next went to Butte City, Montana, and after committing innumerable crimes in that State, I went back again to the State of Washington, and was arrested about eight miles from Spokane Falls for burglary. I was tried, convicted and sentenced once more to two years' imprisonment.

" After the expiration of this sentence I came back to New York City, and for many years continued robbing and stealing over on the West Side. I went into the office of a business man; nobody was there except himself, and I robbed him of all the money he had—something like two thousand dollars. Often, since I gave my heart to God, I have seen that man's face, and I can see the awful look on it as I took the money.

" Shortly after this I met an old thief who knew me and knew of my career, and I told him I was sick and tired of the old life of crime, and he told me about the McAuley Mission, and advised me to come down and see Mr. Hadley. I didn't come until about five days after he told me, but at last I wandered in one evening and asked for Mr. Hadley. The janitor went up and told Mr. Hadley that there was a man downstairs that wanted to speak to him; it was just before

THOMAS FARMER.

WILLIAM H. QUINN.

the evening meeting, and soon Mr. Hadley came down
and spoke to me. He asked me how I felt, and I
told him, and he spoke encouragingly to me, and asked
me if I intended to take Jesus as my Saviour that
night, and I said that I would if I died in the streets
that night. Jesus came into my life that night, and
the past two years have been full of happiness and
sunshine, and I intend to continue in God's work to
the end.

"I feel grateful for all the love and mercy that
have been shown me. Brother Hadley took me here
as janitor; I had no idea that he was going to offer me
this position until I received a letter from him asking
me if I would accept it.

"I was down South at the time with Mrs. Hadley,
and she told me to take it. After that I was made a
leader here on Wednesday nights. I asked Brother
Hadley one day how I was doing on the nights, and he
said: 'You're all right, Tom.' I have had no education but my trust, and day by day He leads me
along.

"If there is a sinner in the house who has ever
been tempted along lines similar to what I have
been, I pray to God that He will make a change to-
night. I want to thank all the friends of this Mission,
and all the converts who have helped me along. I
do not bear animosity against a single person in the
world; I pray every night for all the converts of this
Mission, and I want you to pray for me, and I want
to promise you that I will be kinder and do everything
that lies in my power in the future to help the converts in any way I can.

"I want to thank you sincerely for your kind present to me. I also hope you will continue to help me out on Wednesdays. If I have ever spoken a harsh word to anyone, it is not because of any ill feeling I have towards him, for I do not bear a grudge against a single person, either in this Mission or any place on the earth. I want to lead a good Christian life and do all that I can to win souls for the Master.

"I never knew what a Christian life meant until two years ago. I had spent all my life in crime, scheming how to rob people out of their money, but I want to say now, that so long as I have breath, I will cling to Jesus."

CHARLES S. YATES

"I was brought up in a good Christian home, but unknown to my parents I learned to drink when a mere boy. The habit grew and in early manhood I was a slave to the accursed appetite. For years I tried to conquer it, but could not. At last, having walked the streets night after night from Monday until Saturday, homeless, friendless, despairing, I stood on the corner of Chatham Square, New York.

"Having heard that McAuley Water Street Mission gave lodging tickets to homeless men, I sought out the place for that object alone. Thank God for the reputation of this Mission; for here I heard the Gospel of Christ proclaimed as I had never heard it before. That night God answered my prayer for pardon and I was born again. From that hour no good thing has He withheld. No longer homeless, I have a home where Jesus reigns supreme, a good Christian wife, a dear little boy, and for nearly three years I have had the privilege of spreading the Gospel among seafaring men.   Thank God the only power that can save the drunkard is free to all."

LOUIS W. BROWN

" In the winter of 1887 I was in Philadelphia trying to recover from a drunken debauch, and wandered into a church where B. Fay Mills was holding a series of evangelistic meetings.   I was attracted by the singing. I took a seat in the rear of the church and listened to Mr. Mills, but was not particularly interested until a lame gentleman arose and sang a song, entitled, ' Waiting at the Pool.'   After the song he gave a testimony which strangely affected me, on account of its similarity to my own experience ; it was a testimony which I have heard thousands of times since, and was delivered by S. H. Hadley.   It was the first time I had ever heard anybody admit publicly that he had been a drunkard and a crook, and as I listened to his description of how Jesus came to him in a saloon, detailing in his inimitable way his awful conviction of sin, his experience in the station house to which he went to have himself locked up, and his subsequent conversion in the Jerry McAuley Cremorne Mission, I became deeply convicted of my own sins, and at the close of the meeting when Mr. Mills invited those who were interested in their soul's welfare to remain to an ' after-meeting,' I remained, and when the opportunity was given I arose to my feet and stated how I had been affected by the lame gentleman's testimony.   When I had finished Mr. Hadley arose and made his way to where I was sitting ; he put his arm around me and asked me to wait for him after the service, which I did, and he took me to his hotel.   The next morning he gave me some money and invited me to attend the Mills meetings for a few days, and then come to his Mission at 316 Water Street, New York City, where I was converted about two weeks after my first meeting with Mr. Hadley. I had been an opera singer for several years previous to my conversion, having sung leading baritone parts with different companies in every large city in the United States. I began to drink in moderation and drank and attended to business for years, but alcohol gradually got the better of me; I became unreliable and at last my system became so impregnated with alcohol that I was not normal except under its influence. My wife died of a broken heart, and I sank lower and lower; became estranged from my family, and everything else that was worth having in this world. I signed pledges, made resolutions, but it was all to no avail until I met Mr. Hadley. Since then at different times I have returned to my old profession, against Mr. Hadley's advice, and invariably have fallen; he had repeatedly told me that I would never find a place to rest my feet in the Christian life until I gave up my old profession, and made an unconditional surrender to God of my life and service. He always received me back with open arms, and always believed in me, and said that the Lord had laid me upon his heart, and that he would never give me up. I thank God that he lived to see me rooted and grounded in Jesus. I have been very intimately connected with Mr. Hadley off and on ever since I first met him; have sung for him on his evangelistic trips, and have lived with him in his own home. He was the kindest man I ever knew; he was possessed of that love that we read of in the First Corinthians, thirteenth chapter, ' the love that thinketh no evil, but hopeth all things, believeth all things, endureth all things.' "

MATTHEW J. GALLAGHER

" BROOKLYN, N. Y., May 9, 1906.

" DEAR BROTHER:

" As per your request I send you a brief sketch of my life. It is just one year, six months, fourteen days since I entered the ' old McAuley Mission,' 316 Water Street. I started a Christian life before, but, relying too much on my own strength, and feeling that I could again resume the company of my old companions and keep from drink I did so, forgetting the Mission, and at the same time gradually turning my back upon the truest friend of all sinners, Jesus Christ. It was not long before I again found myself down deeper in the mire of sin than I had ever been before. I began to feel that all hope for me was gone. I determined to give up my old companions, and I did so. I went to the Salvation Army Hotel on Chatham Square, feeling that I might possibly regain my self-respect away from those who were near and dear to me, as well as my old companions. While sitting in the reading-room I got restless; nothing seemed to satisfy me, the spirit of Jesus working on one hand and the devil on the other; it would be useless for me to try to describe the mental anguish I suffered on that occasion. I finally decided to visit the Water Street Mission. I took a seat near the back, thinking that no one would know me. I did not have the least intention of going forward to the mercy seat, as I felt that all hope for me was gone,—I could see nothing before me but a drunkard's grave. When the invitation was given, Brother Wyburn came directly to where I was sitting and asked me to go forward, but I refused. I felt, as I said before, that I was beyond redemption, but after some persuasion I consented to go forward. I must confess it was to please Brother Wyburn, and what a blessing it has been to me since. I surrendered all to Jesus that afternoon, October 23, 1904. I always remember the prayer I offered, which was: ' My dear Jesus, I leave myself in Thy hands, Thy will be done, not mine.' What a wonderful transformation it has been. The Lord has blessed me abundantly in the short space of time I have been converted; I have not found the Christian life a bed of roses, the thorns are there also. Two days after my conversion I had seven hemorrhages; I applied to the Bellevue Hospital for admission, but they were so crowded they could not take me in, but treated me at the dispensary, giving me medicine to take three times a day before meals. I had only one meal a day with the exception of Sundays for two weeks, all this time taking the medicine. I would wait for the whistles to blow, then put the bottle to my lips and take what I thought to be a teaspoonful (I did not have a spoon to take it with). The Lord was good to me on that occasion, as with the odds against me I rapidly regained my health, and to-day can tip the scales at 178 pounds. I thank God for the many friends which He has surrounded me with. I thank Him that it was my great privilege to know Brother S. H. Hadley, whom I learned to love dearly, as I have been his assistant janitor,

and janitor at Wesley, now Hadley Hall on the
Bowery, where I have the pleasure nightly of seeing
many souls won for Jesus. I had known the joy and
happiness of religious life in my younger days; at
sixteen I became a member of the St. Vincent de
Paul Society of the Roman Catholic church, and for
ten years it was my pleasure nightly to go around
among the poor of my district lending a helping hand
and dropping a word of comfort and cheer wherever
I could. Words cannot describe the horror I felt
when I realised that I had become a slave to drink;
I fought it for over seven years, but it seemed that the
harder I fought the lower I descended into sin and
iniquity. I have sometimes walked through the
streets cursing the God that gave me life in one breath
and calling upon Him for mercy in the next. I was
always a firm believer in prayer, and I felt that some
day the Lord would answer my prayer. I thank God
that He did hear and answer my prayer one year,
six months and fourteen nights ago. I have never
wanted to drink since, or to swear or to do a great
many of the things I did in the old life.

"I have found the cure for drunkenness in the
solid rock Jesus Christ. It is my great privilege to
lead the Friday night meeting at Hadley Hall, 293
Bowery, also to have the honour of being the president of the Wesley Brotherhood of the old John
Street M. E. Church, as well as being vice-president of the Blue Button army at Water Street Mission. The way looks brighter as I travel steadily on.
I thank God for the Mission and the life of S. H. Hadley, in that his life was a benediction to me, for he
has taught me to love my fellow-man and lend a help-

ing hand to all who are low down in sin and wickedness. Though the Lord has wonderfully blessed me,
I find that I need Jesus as much in my life to-day as
I did the first day I started out to serve Him. I find
the Christian life is a fight from start to finish, but
thank God, the harder the battle, the sweeter the
victory."

OTTO F. YOUNGS

"Rev. J. WILBUR CHAPMAN, D. D.,
" DEAR FRIEND:
" Our mutual friend, Mr. Wyburn, tells me that you
wish some facts relating to some of the men who
were led from lives of drunkenness and sin, at the
McAuley Mission, 316 Water Street, New York, during the superintendency of the late Mr. S. H. Hadley.
I am one. I was born and brought up here in New
York by Christian parents; had a good home; good
education; fine business prospects; married a fine
girl and had a bright family; and I lost home, love
of children, respect of friends, business opportunities,
my own self-respect, sense of honour, and all that
man holds dear in this world through sin and drink.
I had tried in every earthly way to shake off the hold
that whiskey had upon me,—the so-called gold cures,
etc., but my will power was gone, no human power
seemed to help me. It was a life of ups and downs
until three years, four months and thirteen days ago,
after a prolonged debauch, absolutely homeless, friendless and penniless, right in this great city, where I
was once in an enviable position in every way, unable
to borrow even ten cents, for I had tried to in order
to get a drink and am thankful now that I failed,

for had I got it it might have given me a little temporary courage and I never would have gone into
that Mission; but in the condition stated, and when
no one in the world seemed to have the least particle
of confidence in me,—and I never blamed them,—
I dropped into that God-blessed place. I was tired
and weak for want of food and sleep, and shaking
from debauch. It was about half-past four Sunday
afternoon, December 28, 1902. Mr. Hadley was
there; Mr. Wyburn was giving the invitation after
Mr. Fitzgerald had sung, 'Under His wings I am
safely abiding.' My very soul was touched; all the
good that remained in my poor heart welled up, and
entirely broken in spirit, I went forward, and kneeling at a settee along with three or four other sinners,
I prayed the prayer of the publican. When I arose
Mr. Hadley greeted me, then other gentlemen, and
Mrs. Hadley, Mrs. Lamont and others. I felt a sense
of sin forgiven, and although I had only fifteen
minutes previously been hopeless and ready to plunge
into the river from despair, I had a hope and a
courage such as had not been mine for years. God
had mercifully restored my soul. Mr. Hadley stood
by me and assisted me with money and sympathy and
advice and by his many Christlike examples until I
got on my feet. I and mine thank God for Mr.
Hadley and the McAuley Mission.

"Yours sincerely,
"OTTO F. YOUNGS."

Mr. Hadley's work was of course almost entirely
among men, but his great heart went out to both
lost men and women. As has been said elsewhere,

he searched the newspapers daily to find the names of those awaiting burial and had no friend to weep over them. The following appeared in the New York *World:*

"Instead of a burial among the unknown dead in Potter's Field, the body of the handsome young woman who ended her life by poison in Central Park ten days ago was taken last night to the rooms of the Jerry McAuley Mission in Water Street, where a simple funeral service was held. The body will remain in the undertaking rooms at Nineteenth Street and Eighth Avenue until to-morrow, when it will be buried in Maple Grove Cemetery."

He was also used of God in the conversion of Cora L. Dettinger, and at Mr. Hadley's request she wrote the following as the account of her conversion:

"It is known to many that under God the Water Street Mission has been the greatest blessing of my life, and by God's great goodness I am enabled to recount some of the wonderful things He has done for me while I have been going there. Oh, the guilt, and sin and shame I brought to Him there, and how many a burden, how many a care, and how much sorrow I left there when temptations threatened to overwhelm me, and physical pain and weariness almost made it impossible for me to go on, and when doubts and fears oppressed me and entered my soul, and the devil worked on my weakest points, and held out an easier and pleasanter path, then I flew to my old accustomed place, second bench front, to tell Jesus all about it, and He would make the devil leave me and lift the burden, and angels would come and minister to me, and Jesus Himself would take up His abode in

MR. AND MRS. OTTO YOUNG.

my heart, and gladden and comfort me, and health and strength were given me from on high to help me fight on. But the struggle is over, the fighting done. I have made my unchanging choice for Christ. Victory has been mine and is mine.

"It is known to those who know me that Water Street Mission holds a warm place in my heart, and all feel it right that it should be so. It could not very well be otherwise. To some the place may be dear, to others perhaps precious and blessed, but to me it was even more than that; it was absolutely indispensable to me to persevere in the face of such stupendous obstacles as faced me.

"When I had at length struggled to my feet and secured a position at Child's restaurant, trouble assailed me on every hand. Imagine a girl who has done all she could for twenty years to destroy body and soul (and I well-nigh succeeded), working among people wholly uncongenial to her, to say nothing of the physical and mental strain. Again and again my strength would be taxed to the utmost, and I would be compelled to leave my work, but I was willing to do the most menial task, and bear most anything to retain my hold on Jesus, the tender Saviour, and make a living.

"It looked, however, as though the great sacrifice of Jesus had been in vain after all. A very trying ordeal, for which I was wholly unprepared, nearly swept me off my feet. I had an alarm clock which belonged to a girl who was my chum in the old life. She took it, and I was left without any sort of clock or watch. All my jewelry was left in pawn, and how to be able to rise without an alarm clock was a problem. I was so fretful and worried for fear of not waking up that I could neither sleep nor rest. I had to keep a sort of all-night vigil in order not to be late to my work. It was the custom then for all the girls to change their shirt waists on Thursday. So all unsuspecting of my new difficulty I went to the laundry, when much to my dismay the man informed me that there had been a fire, and in fact he showed me my very own waist, all burned to rags. I told the girl who was over me, and she said, ' To-morrow, then, change,' but where was I to get the waist?

" The idea came to me to wash the one I wore myself, and I had to put it on half damp. I felt so uncomfortable all day and altogether out of sorts from lack of sleep and rest that when I got home I was so disheartened I lost all my courage, and I thought it was not in human flesh and blood to endure more.

" The devil nearly triumphed, for I brought my clenched hand down on my desk and with an oath I swore it had all been a failure. I was a fool for ever thinking I could remain saved and kept, and so I turned my back on the crucified Redeemer, and was about to rush headlong downtown to a place where I spent years in sin. I had reached the steps when a woman on the first floor shouted lustily after me that here was a letter, had been there in fact all day, only she did not hear me come home from work.

" When I looked at that letter I was quite positive I had never seen the scratch of that pen before in my life. I never had. It was from Mr. S. H. Hadley. He quoted this verse to me: Isaiah liv. 10. ' The mountains shall depart and the hills be removed; but my kindness shall not depart from thee, neither shall the covenant of my peace be removed, saith the Lord that hath mercy on thee.' But I found something very substantial besides the verse of Scripture. I felt many things. Here was this letter actually laying there, sent, I believe, by the Lord Himself to cheer and help me, and I all the while getting more irritable, and allowing myself to take my eyes off God even for one minute. I felt so humiliated I went back to my room. It took me a long time to climb the stairs. I could hardly get myself to face God. I was conscious of having wounded and grieved the heart of the Saviour, when He in all thoughtful care stood near me. When I imagined Him to be far off, He was really nearest.

" I picked up my broken lamp which I had knocked off my desk and after spending a long time in prayer I went to bed by a candle light, and so shall I be excused in regarding this Mission with the tenderest affection of which my nature is capable. When I further tell you of its incomparable worth to a life broken and blighted by sin, held in chains which Satan himself wound around me for years, and you could see no way out of it, save to continue the degradation and wickedness, to be delivered and released from such an existence, such a bondage, and having the old hideous sins taken out of your heart and life, and have implanted pure and noble thoughts and inspirations, to which you had been a stranger for years, that would have been enough. I should have been devoutly thankful for so much, and would not have been so greedy as to expect any more, but after redeeming my life from destruction ' He crowned me

with loving kindness' in giving me the friendship
and love of the entire household at 316, and He
lavished 'tender mercies' upon me, for all of which
I am unworthy. In making me a welcome guest
at the Home and table upstairs I thought my cup was
full, but it was filled to overflowing one evening when
we all knelt around the dinner table and Mrs. Lamont
singled me out of the crowd and asked me to pray.

"I have only felt once or twice in my whole life
as I felt then, and I count it the richest experience of
my Christian life to associate and mingle in with these
godly people. What I have seen missing in my own
character I have seen depicted plainly enough in one
of them. That it has been quite easy for me to bring
my own shortcomings and failings to God and ask
Him clearly to put them right, I thank Him from my
deepest heart for all He has made the Mission and
the people I met there to me, but I thank Him even
more that He has claimed me for His child, that I
am His, and that I want to be more like Him every
day I live. He has laid the lost ones on my heart, and
has given me a boundless love and a high ambition to
help those who are so utterly lost and helpless, and it
has actually come to where I can say that I have been
made a blessing to some lives, and I thank Him, oh,
so much, for all that.

"I have often wondered and I have often been
asked, what might, or what could be the hidden, mysterious, secret power back of the great soul-saving
work going on night after night in the Water Street
Mission. Suggestions came and went to my mind,
but I could not arrive at any satisfactory conclusion
until very recently it came to me all of a sudden,

while I was reading the story of the blind beggar, and it is pity, real, true, genuine pity.

"It is an exceedingly rare possession, but it is the great power in Water Street. Love *never faileth*.

"It was manifested in such marvellous degrees by Jesus that the outcast and sick and sinning called Him the Man of Compassion. The suffering blind man never dreamed of such pity. The sinner never looked for, nor imagined such depths of compassion. How Jesus loved, because He first had pity, and pity makes us all tender. When one has the power to pity, you find power to help, comfort and bless.

"When all those sick people crowded around Jesus with their sores and diseases, He looked on them with compassion. He never turned away with disgust, although the demand on Him was ceaseless, but he blessed and healed all. It is so Christlike, the power of pity, and there is such power in it still, for we see it in Water Street practised, and given freely to all who come and ask, and even those who don't ask get an equal share and amount of pity and love and tenderness.

"I ask God to so fill me with pity and love, so as to make me a great blessing to His lost ones, and thus bring great glory to His matchless name."

HARVEY GRAEME FURBAY

A miracle of grace indeed is Dr. Furbay. I knew him in the days of his prosperity, and rejoice in his great conversion. Of Mr. Hadley's influence he writes as follows:

"To speak of S. H. Hadley as my heart prompts or a sense of gratitude suggests, would seem fulsome.

My going to Water Street Mission can never be considered other than a providential direction. Wandering about the city of New York without definite prospect and almost hopeless concerning deliverance from drink, I met accidentally, no, providentially, a young man with whom I had roomed in North Dakota when doing some work for the Board of Publication and Sunday School Work during my junior year in the seminary, 1889. Seeing my condition, he said: 'Why not go down to the McAuley Mission and see Hadley?' Finally I did. When I saw Mr. Hadley and told him my name, he knew who I was. He gave me a substantial meal, and a little money; then asked me if I would pray and I told him that I did not think it was of any use. He said: 'If you feel that way it probably isn't.' He wanted me to come to the meetings. I went once, but was not impressed, did not respond to the invitation extended. Two or three weeks later I went back; no questions were asked, no lecture was given, I was not chided, nor scolded, nor reproached.

"I was almost hopeless. I had been treated for alcoholism in seventeen different institutions. I had prayed. I had isolated myself for weeks and months at a time, all to no purpose. I listened to men giving testimony in Water Street, and gradually hope, new born on the wings of faith, arose in my heart, and I began to pray. I cannot explain it; but without clothing, occupation, friends, or home; separated from and anxious about my two motherless girls, gradually I became contented, lost my anxiety and experienced that peace which comforts with 'Let not your heart be troubled.' I dared not think of the future.

From the many places where I had been treated for inebriety I had come sober, but with no assurance as to the future. When asked if I would refrain from drink, my reply had always been 'I hope so.'

" Within less than ten days after my complete surrender and sincere willingness to do whatever Christ would direct me to do, confidence that He would never leave me nor forsake me took possession of my heart. One trial came to me not many days after giving my first testimony in Water Street. Two clergymen came in and were seated near me, but did not see me. They were men with whom I had spent three years in a theological seminary—my classmates. I did not want to get up and give a drunkard's testimony before them. I reasoned, I have started an honest fight for my life and soul and I will preserve my sincerity. Arising, I gave my testimony, and with it came unexpected strength to my character, and I have never wanted a drink of liquor from that day to this. Mr. Hadley's knowledge of men, their hopes and fears, their struggles and lapses, their environment, nature and habits, gained by experience as drunkard and gambler, and by association as lodging-house keeper on the Bowery and as the dean of rescue mission workers, was so sanctified that he was ' touched with the feeling of our infirmities.' So, his Christlike patience.

" He often said to me : ' Always treat a man so that he will come back to you if he falls.' This accounts for the ' hold he had on men.' A man's past was of no concern to him. A declaration of Christ was sufficient credential. Hadley said : ' That's all God requires. If He is satisfied, I ought to be.'

"His forgiveness was not a mere formal declaration, but an attitude of his nature which the outcast perceived, and at once began to feel the thrill of returning self-respect so essential to stability.

"One day in August, 1905, Mr. Hadley said to me: 'People do not rightly understand the Scripture which says, "Whosoever sins ye remit, they are remitted unto them; and whosoever sins ye retain they are retained." That power is not limited to any person or set of persons. It belongs to me; it belongs to any consecrated believer in Jesus Christ. We forgive men's sins every day in Water Street. We say to the poor broken man: "You have accepted Christ, your sins are forgiven. You are not a drunkard, nor a thief, nor a murderer, but our brother. We believe in you."'

"This spirit, the spirit of the Master manifested when He wrote on the sand, is what held men up to their highest endeavours. From a human standpoint, it is what gave me confidence during the early struggle. This was the spirit with which Mr. Hadley had imbued the Mission. It was not a place of suspicion, but confidence. Men are not watched, but embraced. Queries about possible stability were not entertained. There was no exploiting of one and ignoring another. The coal heaver or 'longshoreman was in the Kingdom of Christ of same honour as the college-bred man or the offspring of some notable family. The communism of the Gospel prevailed,— hence the convert had that best of environment during his early struggles,—brotherly love.

"Mr. Hadley never even remotely suggested the possibility of a man not remaining 'saved.' Therein was manifested the simplicity and sublimeness of his faith; and was supplied strength for the weak in the hour of depression.

" By me, Samuel Hopkins Hadley must ever be remembered as the providential agent through whom I recovered my faith, was redeemed from destructive habits and vices, and restored to activities for which I had been trained and seemed to be endowed."

XX

HIS MONUMENT (Continued)

A FEW years ago the visitors to the Water Street Mission were always impressed by the presence of a grey-haired old gentleman. His testimony was thrilling. One night what he said was taken down and his testimony was sent us.

" Boys," he said, " if you think it's too late for you to be saved, just look at me. I'm getting to be eighty years of age, yet it was only a few years ago that I was picked up, worse off than any of you. It wasn't anything but drink that brought me down. I had a good family and a good wife, but the liquor had a grip on me that nothing could shake. When I found the Lord Jesus Christ, boys, the whole thing passed away like a dream. What was impossible before, was easy then, boys. It don't matter what you think about it now, boys; it'll be just as easy for you, once the love of Jesus takes a hold.

" I began drinking when a boy, my friends—just a little beer and a little wine now and then, but it was the reason of my complete downfall later. At thirty I was a drunkard. I had to sneak away to keep the fact from those who loved me, and I only returned when I knew that I could keep sober for a week or so. Gradually the desire got stronger, and I reached the age of fifty, a sot. I was as hopeless a case as any of you ever saw—worse than any of you are now. Nine times after I was fifty I went to the Kings County Inebriates' Home. There every human means to save me was tried. It was all of no avail. Even the horrors of delirium tremens failed to keep me straight. Boys, I have helped to hold raving crazy men—crazy with the awful torture of delirium tremens; have had them die in my arms, and knowing that the same terrible end awaited me, have gone out and filled myself with rum simply because I couldn't fight it!

" Boys, it was after I had come out of the home for the ninth time that I wandered, shivering and cold, into the Madison Square Park. I had been drunk for days and was a physical and mental wreck. I sat down on a bench and somebody spoke to me. I looked to see who it was, but there was nobody near. Again I heard the voice, and quaking with fear, I went to another bench. The voice followed and then I knew it was my old friend, the delirium tremens.

" Boys, I knew in an hour I would be suffering the tortures of hell. I had just a few minutes to make up my mind what to do. Should I go to the home again? It had never done me more than temporary good. Suddenly I remembered having seen the light of this Mission, having heard the singing through the closed doors, and having once heard a man who was speaking say that Jesus Christ could save anybody. ' I'll go there for a last chance,' I said to myself, ' and, boys, I came here. They took care of me, and though I fell more than once, they brought me to be a good man. It's years since I have touched a drop, boys, and I'll die when my time comes, without again touching the poison. The Lord did it for me, boys, and He'll do it for you."

Now he is unable to be at the Mission, but when he heard that the story of Mr. Hadley's life was being written, he wrote as follows:

"No. 1 Elm St., NEWBURGH, N. Y.
"June 18, 1906.
"REV. SIR AND DEAR CHRISTIAN BROTHER:

"Knowing that you were to write up the life of our precious brother, Hadley, that wonderful missionary to the lost, I thought that it was most fitting that his great helpfulness, untiring sympathy and exhaustless Christian patience in securing my release should be recorded along with those of others.

"My first acquaintance with Brother Hadley occurred some time in 1889, then in my sixty-ninth year: it happened in this wise. Being on the West Side of the city, I strolled into Brother Stephen Merritt's Mission on Franklin Street, bitterly conscious of my rum-ruined condition, which every known means (except the Divine) had failed to relieve. At the conclusion of the services, Brother Merritt furnished me with means and a note to Brother Hadley, at that time managing a lodging house on the Bowery, which I reached about ten o'clock. Brother Hadley had just retired for the night, but after plying the clerk with many persuasive importunities, he finally consented to deliver the note which brought my dear brother from his bed to my aid. He soon joined me in the vestibule of the premises, receiving me with the most cheerful, assuring and loving expression, so natural to him, and took me to a near-by restaurant, where I got the best in the house, with instruction to return to him when through with my supper. Doing so, I found that he had arranged with his clerk for my lodging and food for a time. My nature had become so perverted by the habit of my life that anything beyond the mere gratification of it had no force with me, and whatever else might be done for me, the desire for drink was ever uppermost.

"Having come to know Brother Hadley, I was brought in touch with the dear old Mission in Water Street, coming and going, not yet ready to part with my misery, but oh, the 13th of September, 1890, in my seventieth year, with Brother Hadley and dear Sister Sherwood kneeling beside, I gave my heart to God. He wrote His name thereon, sealed me to Himself. I am now in my eighty-seventh year and the psalm of my life is ' Praise God from Whom all blessings flow ' and the Missions where lost souls may go.

"With sincere Christian love,

"UNCLE REUB. JOHNSON."

JOHN H. WYBURN

Mr. Hadley's assistant for many years in his mission work at Water Street was John H. Wyburn. He was brought out of the darkness of infidelity, and also out of the power of strong drink, into glorious Christian manhood. His devotion to Mr. Hadley could scarcely be put into words. He writes as follows:

"On September 25, 1888, I first met Rev. S. H. Hadley. I shall never forget the first words he spoke to me. I was telling him what I wanted to do (I was in an awful drunken, miserable condition, too drunk to live), to get sobered up, get back to my business, when he said in a very significant tone of voice, ' Is that all you want ? ' I was astonished at his answer, and I thought, ' If you only knew how impossible it is for me to get sober and keep sober,' but in a moment he said with the love and light of heaven in his face, ' What you need, my dear boy, is Salvation, Jesus Christ in your heart; He's the one that will restore to you what you have lost, will restore unto you all things.' He invited me to stay and I did so. Never shall I forget the wonderful testimonies I heard. I thought they were all speaking especially for my benefit. I stood up and said that I wanted some of that! It was a cry for redemption. I knew not what it was at the time, but Jesus knew, bless His dear Name, and on that night the devils were cast out. The old hard heart of unbelief was made new, the cursed appetite for whiskey was taken out of my life.

"From that night Mr. Hadley has been the guiding star of my life; it was he who led me to Jesus, and for over seventeen years, nearly fifteen of which I have had the privilege of being associated with him in this wonderful work, into my heart and life, through his influence, have come the love and pity he had for lost souls who come into the Mission. For over five years I have practically had charge of the work down in Water Street, so far as the spiritual part goes. Mr. Hadley was away the best part of the year,—it was a treat to have him here. Our work had become so great that he was compelled to be absent raising money for the needs of the Mission; but his heart was always here and I believe he is still with us in spirit."

JOHN R. M'CONICA

S. H. Hadley was used not only to assist in leading men to Christ at Water Street, but he was enabled

E. C. MERCER.

JOHN H. WYBURN.

to send many a man out to do rescue work in other cities; such a man is the writer of the following:

"My conversion antedates Brother Hadley's superintendency of the Water Street Mission about one year, having been converted when Mr. John F. Shorey was the superintendent. I was in attendance at the first meeting Brother Hadley conducted in the Mission, and I was the first one Brother Hadley requested to pray at that service. On that occasion I learned to love him very dearly, and as the days went by, my love for him intensified, until I looked upon him almost as a brother in the flesh, as he surely was in the spirit. I am also sure of the fact that he loved me. With Mrs. Hadley he has been a guest at my house when in Montreal, Fall River, Savannah and in Norfolk. I have listened to him as he made me the confidant of many of the secrets of his great soul, baring his heart, and surprising me by the glimpses I thus received of the Christlikeness of his beautiful character. I am indebted to him in every way, for material aid in times of stress financially, and for wise counsels and loving admonitions of a spiritual nature by which I have been 'built up in my faith' and received clearer conceptions of the God-love manifested through the blessed Jesus to me. This memory will ever be an inspiration to me and an incentive to greater efforts for the greater uplifting of those who are 'down and out.' How we (my family and I) miss him. We can scarcely realise, as yet, that he has gone to his reward. Dear Brother Chapman, may all of us so live that 'at the sounding of the trumpet when the saints are gathered home, we shall greet each other by the Crystal Sea.'   "Sincerely your Brother in Christ."

WILLIAM F. ELLIS

"Fifteen years ago I came to New York after I had deliberately thrown a business away. On Sunday night, in a drunken frame of mind in an Eastern city, not very far from here, I took the key of my business, a saloon, and threw it over the transom of the door, and took a midnight train for Baltimore, where I had relatives living; but I made it so unpleasant for them with my drinking habits that they soon got tired of me, and gave me money and a ticket to go back to the city I had come from; like many another fellow I got no further than the Bowery in New York City, and there I began to go down and down, until I finally reached the gutter. Time and time again I had to be sent to institutions for drunkenness, but all to no avail. On the night of November 10, 1903, God in His infinite goodness touched my guilty soul in the dear old McAuley Mission and set me free, and thank God I have been free ever since. If God had only saved me from the appetite for strong drink, I would even then be a most happy man, but I never knew what genuine happiness was until I got the grace of God deeply rooted in my heart. The dear Master has given me love for others that are down in the horrible pit and miry clay like I once was, and He has also restored my darling little daughter to me, who was lost to me for about six years. There is only one thing in my life that I wish for now, and that is to know more of Him who died for me. Praise His Holy Name."

W. H. QUINN

From Hell to Heaven

" There was no time in my life that I did not know the taste for liquor. One of the first things that I remember is drink and its surroundings. As a child I just loved the taste of it and was ever ready and willing to go for a can of beer or a bottle of whiskey. I well remember how I would take a drink in the hall and then look for more in the house. So I had an early start on the road that would surely land me in hell. Unlike most boys, I had no early Christian training or Sunday School teachings. I have often testified that I came into this world, and then became like the people I grew up among,—a drunkard and a crooked man. At the age of fourteen I had already been arrested and in court twice. As I grew older and had a taste of prison life, the longing came over me many times to lead a different life. How well I remember on Sunday morning, seeing well-dressed, smiling, happy people going and coming from church, and I wished that I was like them. At that time I thought it was because they had friends, and home, and money, that they looked so happy. Then I would go and do something wrong to get money, and that would mean more whiskey and more misery. When I wanted whiskey I would stop at nothing to get it. I remember one Sunday afternoon while walking along the streets half crazy from Saturday night's debauch, I came to a saloon, in the window of which was a display of bottles of whiskey. The very sight of these was like putting a match to dynamite, and I broke in that large plate glass window and taking several quart bottles of the whiskey ran and got away with them. I do not think it would have been safe for anyone to have attempted to stop me that Sunday. I kept going from bad to worse. Of course, there were times when locked up, that I had no whiskey, and at such times I would say, ' When I get out of here, I will disappear. I will go to another city where no one knows me and get work, stop drinking and be an honest, respectable man.' But it was of no use. I could not change my way of living. I knew no other life, yet I longed to be good. Then I enlisted in the United States regular army, thinking that the discipline, etc., there would lead me at least to live a straight life. But there I was soon regarded as crooked, and I did not like that name, among over eight hundred men. Before long I had had my first court-martial, and several others followed with guard-house sentences. Coming back from the funeral of the late President McKinley, my company being there on duty, I got on a frightful drunk, and when my money was all gone, I borrowed all that I could, sold all my clothes, got trusted for as much whiskey as I could, and *then* I was not through. I still wanted drink and I got *it,* and the police got *me.* I committed a crime at night that enabled me to satisfy for a time my craving for drink, and a few days later I was arrested, tried and again was behind the bars. Then my discharge was mailed to me from the Army. It read: ' Discharged without honour for being held by civil authorities.' While in that prison one day, a Christian lady asked me where I was going when released; where was my home? I told her I was going to get away from that part of the country. I did not know

WILLIAM F. ELLIS.

WILLIAM BRUCE.

where to go, I had no home, I *had* nothing, I *was* nothing. In time I reached New York and got work several times, but could not keep it. So I slept in parks and on docks, living off ' free lunch' bars. But I did not ' live,' I merely existed until September 25, 1902. That day in a half-dead condition in a saloon on Park Row, New York City, not knowing what to do, another drunkard asked me where I was ' putting up.' I told him I was holding down that pier at the foot of Twenty-fourth Street. He said: ' How long are you in New York?' I replied: ' A few months.' When he learned that I did not know where Water Street Mission was and that I did not know Mr. Hadley, he told me that I was ' slow'; then he began to teach me a new way of getting a living without work. He said: ' This Mr. Hadley used to be a drunkard, and now he wants to help the man that is down and out. So you get as drunk as you can and go down to the Mission, and if you are only foxy you can work that place all winter. When you are through there, I will give you a list of other places.' That night found me in the Mission, with no good intentions in my heart. The man who was with me asked me how much I was going to touch Mr. Hadley for, and what story I would give him. I replied: ' I can't tell until I size him up.' I do not know anything about the first part of the meeting, only when a man had finished his solo I wanted to applaud and bring him out again. I had never been in a mission before. But when men stood up and testified that they knew all about the life that I was living because they had lived it, and told how Jesus had come into their lives, and had taken away all desire for whiskey and wrongdoing, then I was awake. One man said that only two weeks ago he was a drunkard in the gutter and Jesus had saved him. I sprang to my feet and said, ' I want to be like those fellows.' I was told to sit down and I would get a chance later on; the man that was with me said I was getting crazy; when the invitation was given to those who wanted to start in the new life—the Christian life—I was one of the first to come forward, and as I knelt there I forgot all that man had told me about ' working ' the mission. It just seemed like the Holy Spirit came into my life and illuminated my darkened understanding, and made it very plain to me *why* I was a homeless drunkard and a crooked man. It was because I was a sinner. So I knelt at Jesus' feet with a sincere desire in my heart to get away from a sinful life. I was asked to pray, but did not know how. Then I was told to say, ' God be merciful to me, a sinner, for Jesus' sake.' I did so, and because I was sorry for my sins and meant business and wanted to know this Jesus that the men told me about, God heard and answered my prayer. Praise His Name. Now I want to be like Him, for He has taken out of my life all desire for whiskey, lying, stealing, and in fact, every evil that was in my old life. ' Old things have passed away and all things have become new.' How I want to tell out the glad news of the power of God to save and keep such as I was. There is seldom a day but there is someone to whom I tell of the power of God to save all that come unto Him. One day a minister told me about a man whose wife was a member of his church. He was often drunk, and the dear wife with a breaking heart would ask this pastor to do something for him. But he did not know what to do. He said, ' When a man is drunk I know it is no use talking to him, and when he is sober, I have not the courage.' Right here I believe God used me. For I told this good man that God could save a man when drunk as well as when sober, and told him of several men who came to the Mission and knelt down drunk, and got up sober and, praise God, have been sober ever since. He said, ' I am glad I met you and had this talk. The next time this man is drunk I am going to get him on his knees.' Indeed, he seemed somewhat anxious that he would get drunk *soon;* that he might tell him that Jesus could remove the desire for whiskey from him forever.

" Two days after the Lord saved me He gave me a good job, and I have made an honest living for almost four years. I think I get more out of this salvation than most people I hear testify. They tell how God has restored to them the things that Satan had robbed them of; how they fell from a high social position, etc. Well, I had never been up to come down.

" But now God has blessed me with things I never dreamed of, things that I never had. Now I go to church, and am happy like those I once envied. All because I belong to Jesus. Neither tongue nor pen can express what Mr. Hadley's life and teaching and influence have been to me. God used him to make me comprehend what there is to enjoy in the Christian life. I thank God for nearly four years of close fellowship with this man of God. I am enlisted now in the Army of the Lord, and when my enlistment is up and the bugle calls me to my Saviour, the Commander-in-Chief, I want an honourable discharge, and a place with Him in His Kingdom. What God has done for me, He can do for anyone, no matter how low down, if they will only come to Him and mean business."

THOMAS C. MILLERICK

How a rebel became a regular by the instrumentality of Samuel Hopkins Hadley.

"Born in New York City, the first remembrance I have of my being was at my mother's knee, where she taught me my evening prayer, and then she would lift me up and place me in her lap, and sing the old familiar hymns,—one I distinctly remember, ' Oh, Happy Day that Fixed My Choice,' and after singing she would talk to me. I now believe she was praying about me, and asking God to take care of her boy. Thank God for such recollections, which money could not buy if they could be sold. When I was about five or six years old she took me to a Methodist Sunday School, and while she left me in the infant class, she attended the Class Meeting; after classes were over, we went upstairs, to the church service. This is the life I lived and was brought up to until I was about sixteen years old. Mother had died one year previous, and father just three years later. After mother's death I had my own way the greater part of the time, stayed out late at night, went to theatres, balls, picnics, and places of such kind. I was not content at school, so I secured employment with a banking house in this city. I remained eight years with this house, during which time I had the brightest prospects of making a name for myself in a business way, yet ' What shall it profit a man if he gain the whole world and lose his own soul?' But I neglected the early training and went into sin by seeking the pleasures of this world.

"When about seventeen years of age I found myself on the race track, and I became infatuated with the game, so much so that I robbed my employers, pawned any and everything obtainable to get money to bet. At first I made money—for three or four years—and never thought I would be in want of a dollar, or a friend, but alas, alas, the things of this world are fleeting. During these few years I had learned to drink, for then I looked upon it as a manly act to be able to drink whiskey. The habit grew and grew, from just liking it to an appetite which I could not control.

"Once I stood at the bar drinking in a fashionable café, which I was accustomed to frequent, when the bartender, noticing that whiskey had a hold on me, said, 'Young man, if you stick to that stuff you will wear old clothes.' I laughed at him, thinking he was joking, and again he said, 'If you do, you will remember my words.' I shall never forget them, and wish I could burn them in letters of fire before every young man who is just beginning to drink intoxicating liquors, not because it brings old clothes, but because of hell, and lost condition of soul it brings.

"From that time on I gradually went down, and it took me about ten years to get to the bottom. This incident in my life was brought home to me shortly after my conversion in the Water Street Mission, by the words which are painted on the wall, 'The drunkard shall come to poverty.'

"It would be impossible for me to describe what

I went through those ten years, each year growing weaker and weaker, as to being able to recover myself. At first given good advice by friends and employers, I was helped in every way possible until they finally had to drop me with the words, ' He is no good, he is no good.' I secured position after position, only to lose them by the appetite which mastered me. My home was broken upon two different occasions, and my relatives left me to the doom which was before me,—at last a wanderer, and an outcast.

" I often asked myself the question why I was born to live such a hell on earth and often wished I was dead. I would seek the most secluded spots I could find, such as docks, parks, and the outskirts of the city, so that I would not be seen by those who knew me.

" In the daytime I was longing and wishing for the night to come, and in the night wishing for the day to come, hungry, tired, and hopeless of ever getting away from such a life. Oh! the life of a drunkard, so filled with remorse and anguish, which cannot be described.

" At this period of my life I often wandered into missions ' to pass the time away,' in sleeping or getting warm,—often impressed with the service, but only to go out again to wander, and think ' what is going to become of me?' Why I did not embrace Christianity at this time I cannot say, unless it was that I was not ready to give up a worldly life, with all its misery. I wanted to be sober, but thought there was no happiness in a Christian life. What a mistake! The only true happiness and peace is found in living a Christian life. I am glad I am a Christian to-day;

I am glad I am alive, for life with Christ is heaven upon earth. Towards the end of this downward career I would do and have done almost anything to obtain money to satisfy my desires and appetites, and have taken some desperate chances, so much so that if I had been caught by the authorities, I could have been sent away for a long term of years, and yet I was never charged by the law with any greater crime than drunkenness, for which I am grateful.

" On Saturday, January 22, 1898, I was discharged from a position for drunkenness and dishonesty, a politer way of putting it than calling one's self a thief. With my salary in my pocket I went to a saloon and there remained playing cards until the time of closing, which was midnight. More or less under the influence of whiskey, four of us adjourned to one of the players' rooms, where we continued to play until six o'clock Sunday morning. Then I arose from the table, stone broke, and commenced to drown my sorrow in more whiskey, and succeeded in that, for I slept off two drunks that day. My last recollection of the afternoon was at two o'clock. When I awoke I was in the Water Street Mission about seven o'clock, Sunday evening, January 23, 1898.

" Where I was or had been since the early afternoon I cannot tell, nor can I tell how or when I got into the Mission because of the utter intoxication I was in. Here ends the first chapter of my life as a drunkard, or rebel.

" But I will never be able to write by pen or convey in speech the second chapter as a Christian, or regular, until I see Jesus and thank Him for redemption and for bringing Samuel Hopkins Hadley into my life.

I was asleep as dear Brother Hadley came into the Mission. He saw me and wakened me, saying, 'Is this one of the regulars?' No, I was not; as my life story indicates, I was a rebel, and had lived in open rebellion against God's Kingdom all my life until that night. Brother Hadley has often said, 'Some men will sleep themselves into hell,' and that was just what I was doing after my debauch.

"The meeting was now beginning with song and prayer. One song I remember:

"'I stood outside the gate, a poor wayfaring child,
    Within my heart there beat a tempest loud and wild;
    A *fear* oppressed my soul, that I might be *too late*
    And, oh, I trembled sore, and prayed outside the gate.'

"Then I heard testimonies of redeemed drunkards, and it seemed to sober me somewhat, for they were telling over and over my life story, and they said that Jesus had saved them out of it and they were now living Christian lives, and they were happy and prosperous, and furthermore they said this Jesus would do the same for anyone that came to Him. I believed these men.

"Mr. Hadley at the close of the meeting said, 'It was on Sunday evening that I was born again.' He wanted to know if there was anyone in the room that wished to be born again, and live a Christian life and start for heaven, and then said if there was anyone, to stand on his feet.

"I accepted the invitation by springing to my feet, so eager was I that night to die to the old life. He then invited those who stood to come forward and kneel down and pray. Eleven men responded. I was somewhat dazed from the effects of my debauch, and really did not know what to say or pray for, but Brother Hadley said, ' Pray " God be merciful to me a sinner, for Jesus' sake." ' I did so, and I am glad to say that God heard the prayer and answered it by redeeming me from a sinful life. After we prayed Mr. Hadley asked us to make a statement. We all said something. I told him I had prayed God be merciful to me a sinner and that I believed He had done so, and I have been believing it ever since. Brother Hadley then took us by the hand and wished us God-speed in the new life.

" As I was leaving the Mission that night very much sobered up, I was met at the door by a lady. She greeted me with a smile and a warm shake of the hand. I afterwards knew her as Mrs. Bentley, the missionary. She asked me to come back the following evening, but to trust God for the future. How vague those words sounded then, but now I understand them, and no good thing has He withheld from me.

" This yielding myself to God was as wonderful a conversion as St. Paul's, for in my mad career previous to finding myself in the Mission I was not thinking of God, of Jesus, Church, or Mission. My one thought for days had been to get away from relatives, friends and self by going across the continent to Frisco, Cal., but God works in a mysterious way His wonders to perform, and while I thought I was very far from Him, He was very near to me, and He brought me to Himself. Oh, what a change in my life from that night! Words are inadequate to express the joy, peace, and happiness I have experienced in the knowledge of sins forgiven and Sonship of God.

"The Christian life I had to live all over again just like a little child. I did not even remember the Lord's Prayer, and the Bible was a sealed book to me, just like so much Greek.

"The Monday morning after my conversion when I awoke, I did not want a drink, something unusual in my life, especially after a debauch. I then recalled the happenings in the Mission the night before, and began to believe that I was saved, for I did not want a drink that day, nor for months and months after. Since that time a work of grace has been going steadily on in my life until the old life has completely passed away, and new desires and ambitions are now filling its place. Surely, 'if any man be in Christ, he is a new creature.' During the first and second year of the new life I was weak in the faith, and on several occasions temptation overcame me and I fell back in the old ways for a few days, but only to return penitent and with a stronger determination to live a Christian life to the end. And the dear Lord by His Holy Spirit has led me along thus far to know that 'Christ is all in all.'

"About eight weeks after my conversion I secured employment, the same which I hold at present, by the grace of God. He gave my employer confidence in me and since then I have held a responsible position. Not long after that friends, relatives and home were again what they used to be in bygone years. I united with a church, the same church where I attended Sunday School. I became an active member, then a steward and a little later those good people saw fit to make me their class leader. When they are going to stop bestowing their love upon me I do not know, but one thing I do know, the happiest days of my boyhood were spent in this church, and thank God I am now enjoying them over again, with the blessed consciousness that it is all real, very real. 'The grace of God it is so sweet.' Brother Hadley made me a co-worker with him at the Mission, appointing me a leader with the blessed privilege of inviting sinful men to Jesus. What joy it gives one to see His double returning home again to the Father to wander no more; to see him changed and in his right mind, after receiving power over the old life, and receiving the good things which God has in store for them that trust Him.

"During these years I have learned much from Brother Hadley. As he lived Christlike he has been an example, a teacher and a guide to me, always offering words of encouragement and comfort. I can now say he was more interested in my welfare than I have been myself.

"Can I ever thank God enough for Samuel Hopkins Hadley, and for his disturbing me in my drunken sleep, which by so doing has brought me new life, salvation and heaven right here?

"Hallelujah! for freedom to-day from whiskey, tobacco, and everything that is wicked and bad."

XXI

NEWSPAPER COMMENT

NOT a very great while ago one of the most distinguished politicians died. He was formerly a member of the President's Cabinet and had rendered invaluable service to his country along political lines. He was truly a great man and yet the newspaper comments concerning his passing away from his political career were not for a moment to be compared with the references in the public press, both secular and religious, to the life and work of S. H. Hadley, whose mission in life was to help uplift others from whom the world, and alas, too often, even the Church had turned away.

The editor of the *Westminster*, Dr. Richard S. Holmes, has placed in verse his tribute to Mr. Hadley:

A broken reed on which no life could lean:
    A bit of floatsam tossed on hostile shore:
    A human wreck was he, and nothing more.
Sometimes the thought of what he might have been
Fell on his soul. As snowflakes on the green
    In late spring days, when winter's rule is o'er
    Whiten a moment, then pass open door
Of waking earth into the vast unseen:—
So fell the thought on this poor ruined soul
    But left no impress for a future good.
And then the change,—"Christ Jesus makes thee whole."
    Grew straight the broken reed: the wave-tossed wood
Became a waymark: and the wreck a guide
To souls adrift out on Sin's whelming tide.

Under the heading, "A Dramatic Religious Career," the *Literary Digest* says:

"There is a certain dramatic appeal to the imagination in the story of a direct descendant of the relentless theologian, Jonathan Edwards, who gradually sinks from respectability and well being until he is a hopeless drunkard, a gambler, a thief, and ultimately that forlorn wreck known as a 'bum,' and is then lifted from the depths to a life of such efficiency that at his death it is seriously affirmed from one pulpit that he 'was the greatest American of his time—not measured in money or in fame, but in love and in likeness to Christ.' Such is the story of the Rev. Samuel Hopkins Hadley, for more than twenty years at the head of the old Jerry McAuley Mission in Water Street, New York."

Dr. Arthur T. Pierson, in the *Missionary Review of the World,* says:

"I have never known the equal of Samuel Hopkins Hadley as a winner of souls. In his death the Christian Church has experienced the greatest loss in this respect in half a century."

Dr. James M. Buckley, in the *Christian Advocate,* New York, says:

"Mr. Hadley's inexhaustible patience appears in what he was wont to say of his methods, 'If a man cheats me nineteen times, I shame him out by trusting him the twentieth.' As a man he was of more than ordinary ability—his imagination was vivid, vocabulary large and of good quality, his susceptibility and suggestibility great, his wit unusually bright, his sympathies easily excited, and he was master of the art of good-fellowship. Down to the depths he sank; up from the depths he rose; regenerated and moved upon by the Spirit he ' felt the infirmities ' of those he would help. More than that, he loved them."

The following are grouped from the *Literary Digest:*

" ' He has been a power for good beyond the possibilities of just estimation,' says the New York *Examiner;* and we are told elsewhere that he so quickened the work of Jerry McAuley's Mission that leaders of religious thought and sociological students from all parts of the world came to the humble headquarters at Water Street to learn of him. ' The work of this unique mission,' states the *Episcopal Recorder,* ' was carried on by converts, who were once thieves, tramps, sandbaggers, or drunkards, and they have proved themselves workmen that need not to be ashamed.' Mr. Hadley used to say that more thieves and drunkards had crossed the threshold of the Mission than that of any other building in the city, except the Tombs Prison."

The Philadelphia *Press* says:
" The good man never dies.
" So ' Hopp ' Hadley is dead, and one of the country's greatest philanthropists has fallen.
" Yes, ' great philanthropist '; it is not the man who gives millions that he will never miss, to keep his own name blazoned forth in perpetuity, upon some public building, that is the true philanthropist. Philanthropy, as everyone who knows words understands at a

glance, does not mean money-giving; it means humanity-loving. A man may be a lover of his kind and prove it, yet not know where his own next month's rent is coming from.

" It is possible to be a penniless philanthropist; and it is also possible to be a million-dollar-giving enemy of the race.

" ' Hopp' Hadley, as a wide diversity of friends affectionately styled him, because of his limp; Samuel H. Hadley, as the records run, loved his fellow men with an intensity, a quenchless hopefulness; and a tireless helpfulness marked him as one of the saviours of his time. At close grips and at personal cost he served mankind. No dilettante æsthetic he, toying with the problem of poverty and wretchedness as a drawing-room diversion. He went straight down to the mire where the outcasts lie, and in spite of dirt and drink and ingratitude, and all manner of unloveliness, he persisted in lifting men up.

" Most social reformers would go out of business in a week if they had to touch with their own white hands the actual men and women who make up the problems which they study.

" It was a great gratitude and a great love which made Hadley an ' apostle to the drunkard.' Many Philadelphia audiences have heard him tell the story of his life, which was also the story of the Water Street Mission, New York, for twenty years past. In his own picturesque speech, which to the end retained the flavour of the Bowery twenty-four years ago, he was ' down and out '—a drunkard, a forger, an outcast, a ' bum.' Delirium tremens had all but completed the wreck of mind and body. Suddenly he made a resolution while sitting in a Harlem dive, a home-less, penniless sot, that he would quit drink and the old life. Alas, his will power was gone, and he had made the same determination many times before. On this occasion he had an illumination: He would have himself locked up. And he did. There in a narrow cell thronged with all the imps that haunt the drink-crazed, he underwent a religious experience which transformed his life almost beyond belief. Every year since then, on the anniversary of his conversion, he has gone back to that station house, and in the same cell he has had a little prayer meeting by himself.

" There is no measuring the might of a man with a tremendous purpose.

" The ex-crook, ex-drunkard, ex-' bum,' gave himself to the work of lifting up the men who are still as low as he had been. On the East Side of New York he found no lack of material. The romance of his life lies in the fact that hundreds of men in honourable places to-day, their past all unsuspected by their present associates, were helped out of the Bowery gutters by this indomitable optimist. This means more than the commonplace fact that among the thousands of poor wrecks whom Hadley succoured there were men from every corner of America and the whole world, who once had borne honourable names; for even the highest may fall to the lowest, ' Facilis descensus Averni.' But the climb from a Harlem dive to the heights of respectability and honour and usefulness is a rugged and romantic way.

" This man Hadley knew that it was possible for the lowest to be lifted up; his reason was the best in the world; he had gone through the experience himself. So his patience with the weak and the will-less, the indifferent, and the mere pretenders, was nothing short of divine. I heard him tell in the Garrick Theatre one day of a 'bum' to whom he had given shelter, who straightway stole his overcoat. But that didn't interfere with his welcome the next time he could be reached. Time after time the poor drunken rogue played his benefactor false. But Hadley lived to see that particular wretch become an upright, useful man.

"There will be no imposing mausoleum to hold Hadley's body; but thousands of men are scattered over the earth, walking in their integrity, monuments to his life.

"Illiterate, yet the author of a heart-gripping book that has sold twenty thousand copies; unpolished in speech, yet moving audiences of thousands of educated persons; unequipped with a theological education, yet able to preach with a power which few doctors of divinity ever attain; honoured by the great and yet unspoiled and ever impatient to be back in the Bowery with his 'bums,' for whom he prayed with his last gasp—such was this mighty philanthropist, S. H. Hadley, superintendent of the Jerry McAuley Mission, 'down in Water Street,' New York. Few kings have had such a funeral cortege as he; for the poor, the outcast, the drunken and the criminal of a great city knew him as a friend and helper.

"The greatest usefulness is the greatest success: 'Hopp' Hadley was more successful than hundreds of millionaires.

"Passersby wondered what it meant to see a silent

stream of 400 men and women walk rapidly down under Brooklyn Bridge, stop before a modest little building on Water Street and then crowd into a little room not half big enough to hold then. The reason for this was that nearly everybody that had met Samuel H. Hadley there in the last nineteen years wanted to look once on his dead face and to tell of his living acts. There was little time for these oral testimonies during the brief funeral services. One convert, the first, repeated his story, and some of the business men who have helped to make possible the unbroken usefulness of the Old Jerry McAuley Mission told how the sincerity of this man's life had won their absolute confidence. Many of the onlookers wept silently.

"Outside, the tugs in the East River whistled. A band played for an Italian funeral two blocks away. The picks of the street cleaners in the hard snow clacked against the pavement. Nobody minded these things. It was all a part of the life Sam Hadley belonged to. Somebody asked, after it was all over with, where were the converts of the mission—those ragged, blear-eyed hulks.

"'Why, these are all respectable, clean-looking men!' exclaimed the visitor.

"'They are—now. That is what Sam Hadley was good for.'"

The *New York Tribune* says:

"A good man is gone and a great loss is suffered by the world in the death of Samuel Hopkins Hadley. 'When our names are blotted out and our place knows us no more,' said Huxley, 'the energy of each social service will remain, like the unending stream of one of nature's forces.' There is no incongruity in comparing the energy of Hadley's social service with that of even some of the greater of nature's forces. It is said, probably without exaggeration, that at his meetings at the Water Street Mission in those last twenty years no fewer than seventy-five thousand persons declared their intention to lead better lives. There is reason for confidence that a majority of these were true to their resolutions. Surely, to have rescued thousands of lives from beggary, vice and crime and to have made them industrious and law-abiding members of the community is such a service to the state as not many other men have performed. To have saved a large number of souls from death is, from the spiritual point of view, a service of simply immeasureable greatness.

"But that was by no means all. It was directly through his influence that his brother became interested in Christian beneficence and became the leader of a large mission and the founder of some forty others; that the three sons of that brother also entered the same field of usefulness; and that many other men —most of them converts in the Water Street Mission —became the heads of Christian and benevolent enterprises. Thus his influence was through all those years not only widening in its own circle, but it was establishing other centres from each of which similarly widening circles of good works proceeded, and each of which in turn created yet other centres, and so on.

"The sum total of the good thus done by this one devoted man is something that cannot be computed. It would be impossible to reckon how much it has amounted to just to the present time. But now Hadley's work has only just begun. It ' will remain,' like the unending stream of one of nature's forces.

" There are those who lament the decline of faith and the decadence of the churches. What a tremendous rebuke to such does the career of a man like Samuel Hopkins Hadley present! For the main-spring and motive of his life, its Alpha and Omega, was Christian faith—' the feeling that there's a God, He reigns and rules.' A Methodist in technical church membership, purely undenominational in his mission work, he had the same faith that Bunyan, and Baxter, and Wesley had, and that his own famous ancestor, Jonathan Edwards, had. He had precisely that ' old-fashioned religion ' that so many of our churches deplore the decline of and fitfully seek to restore. He had it, and the power of it worked in and through him as surely, as unmistakably, and as effectually as ever it did through any of the canonised spiritual leaders of the past. And he himself would have been the most earnest in denying, and denying truthfully, that he was any rare or unique exception to the rule. What he did others could do. The church or the minister lamenting the unfruitfulness of its or his work should regard this example, and learn from it that failure to effect results comparable with Hadley's simply argues failure to cherish the faith that he cherished and practised, to make the consecration of effort that he made, and spend the love that he spent."

The New York *Herald* devoted an entire page of the Sunday edition of the paper in which a tribute was paid to Samuel Hopkins Hadley, who was spoken of as "The Foe of Iniquity." The reporter wrote as follows:

"If there is joy in heaven over one sinner that repenteth and turns but himself from evil ways, how much must there be when that one not alone sets forth upon the straight and narrow path, but takes with him legions of others, and that not by Scriptural exhortation or empty homilies on the abstract advantages of virtue, but by practical help, by giving food to the hungry and shelter to the homeless, whatever the degree of their iniquity, by sacrifices, abnegation and devotion.

"Some there were, perhaps, who knew that he was superintendent of the old Jerry McAuley Mission at No. 316 Water Street, but how many of these could tell you even now exactly what that Mission is and what was accomplished under his care and direction. Fewer still, only a small band of those who had watched and profited by his career, could tell you that he was one of the most remarkable men of his time, because he possessed not only those great qualities of soul which marked his illustrious progenitor Jonathan Edwards, but manifested them by deeds which, however mean or sordid they may seem in the recital, are glorified and illumined in their meaning and their consummation.

"Not only himself, but fully seventy-five thousand others, Hadley raised from the depths of sin and degradation and set upon the ways of decency. But to be understood the story must be told from his own beginning. Born in Malta township, Morgan county, Ohio, in 1842, he was not only a direct descendant of the great Calvinistic preacher of Enfield, but his mother was the daughter of a clergyman and his mother's brother also was a clergyman. His early boyhood and young manhood were spent in a log house built by his father, and his formal education was acquired in about four months in a log schoolhouse.

"In his later days, speaking of his early home, he used to say: ' It was the purest spot on earth. Never did I hear an evil word spoken there, and no whiskey or tobacco ever passed the sacred threshold of our log cabin home. As early as I can remember I had promised my mother that I would never drink, and I kept this promise until my eighteenth year.'

"He drifted to New York in 1870 and obtained a position with a salary of $300 a month and a liberal allowance for expenses, but the failure of the establishment he was working for threw him out, and never again was he able to command a good salary. Downward he kept slipping, until he learned to know the horrors of what he called a ' drunkard's hell.'

" ' Talk about hell,' he said, long afterward, ' I tell you I know what it is, and any man who has been along that line knows that I tell the truth. The Bible describes hell as the place where the rich man, being in torment, lifted up his eyes and saw Abraham afar off and Lazarus in his bosom. Then the rich man begged for one drop of water to cool his parched tongue, for he was tormented in this flame.

" ' My idea of hell, from the experience I have had, is that it is a place shut off, where all hope is lost, where purity and love are strangers, and anguish of the most poignant kind has taken possession of the soul. That was what I felt the night I fled from a

WESLEY, NOW HADLEY HALL.

saloon—fled for my life to a police station and had myself locked up.

"'Love is heaven and when love has fled from the human heart then hell begins. I had lost my friends. I could not get five cents without stealing it. Then came delirium tremens, creeping stealthily upon me. Demons of the mist in hideous forms danced before my horrified gaze. I closed my eyes, but I could not shut them out. They danced closer and closer, until their scorching breath burned me. Serpents twined about my throat, choking me, and on all sides I heard sneering, mocking voices plotting my ruin. Then a lower voice came, whispering with shrill distinctness: "Kill yourself! You have played for this for years. You are mine now. Kill yourself!"'

"How that night passed, he said, he never could tell, but in the morning he went to the home of his brother, Colonel H. H. Hadley, who afterwards founded the Church Army of the Protestant Episcopal Church. On the following Sunday evening he went to the Jerry McAuley Cremorne Mission, in West Thirty-second Street, and put himself in the hands of McAuley, who had been a river thief. He asked Jerry to pray for him, but the reply was: 'All the prayers in the world won't save you unless you pray for yourself.'

"Later, in his brother's home, he felt that the help which he had craved had been given and he believed that he had been converted. From that time he attended the services with such regularity that he was virtually an inmate of the place, and, finally, four years later, in 1886, the trustees of the Mission asked him to become its superintendent. He did so, and remained there the rest of his life, with no other devotion, as he expressed it, than to be 'the friend of the down and outs.'

"'More thieves and drunkards,' he used to say, 'have crossed the threshold of the Mission than any other spot in the city except the Tombs prison. Water Street is a place where drunken men are more welcome than the sober, the thief more welcome than the honest man, the fallen woman more welcome than the virtuous one. If a man comes to our Mission without shoes we give him a pair. That is the policy of our Mission.

"Those were the principles upon which this remarkable man conducted the old Mission down in the slums under Brooklyn Bridge. The entire work of the place was carried on by the converts, men who had once been highway robbers, tramps, and drunkards. Absolutely undenominational, Jew and Gentile, Catholic as well as Protestant, were welcome to its benefits. There is love enough for all, was Hadley's doctrine, and if a man who is 'down and out,' only shows a true desire to be 'up and in,' the workers are well rewarded, and he may choose for himself the Church agency which he thinks will be most satisfying and supporting to his new desires.

"In the years of service in Water Street not less than seventy-five thousand persons have announced their intention to live better lives. Not all of these have stood firm in the new faith, of course, but it is safe to say that the percentage has been as large as, if not larger than, would be the case following an ordinary revival. Men of all nations and of all professions and trades have begun there life anew. One of the wealthiest citizens of Australia, who is at the head of a great system of rescue work in Australia and New Zealand, calls the Water Street Mission his 'mother church.' Dr. John H. Kellogg, head of the Chicago Lifeboat Mission and other rescue agencies, refers to it as 'my inspiration,' and only recently the vice-president of one of the great railroads in the South, recalled that there was a time when he had been one of Hadley's 'bums.'"